ONE FOCUS

The Journey to Finding Your Peaceful Purpose

Dr. Latizzia Bragg-Bullock

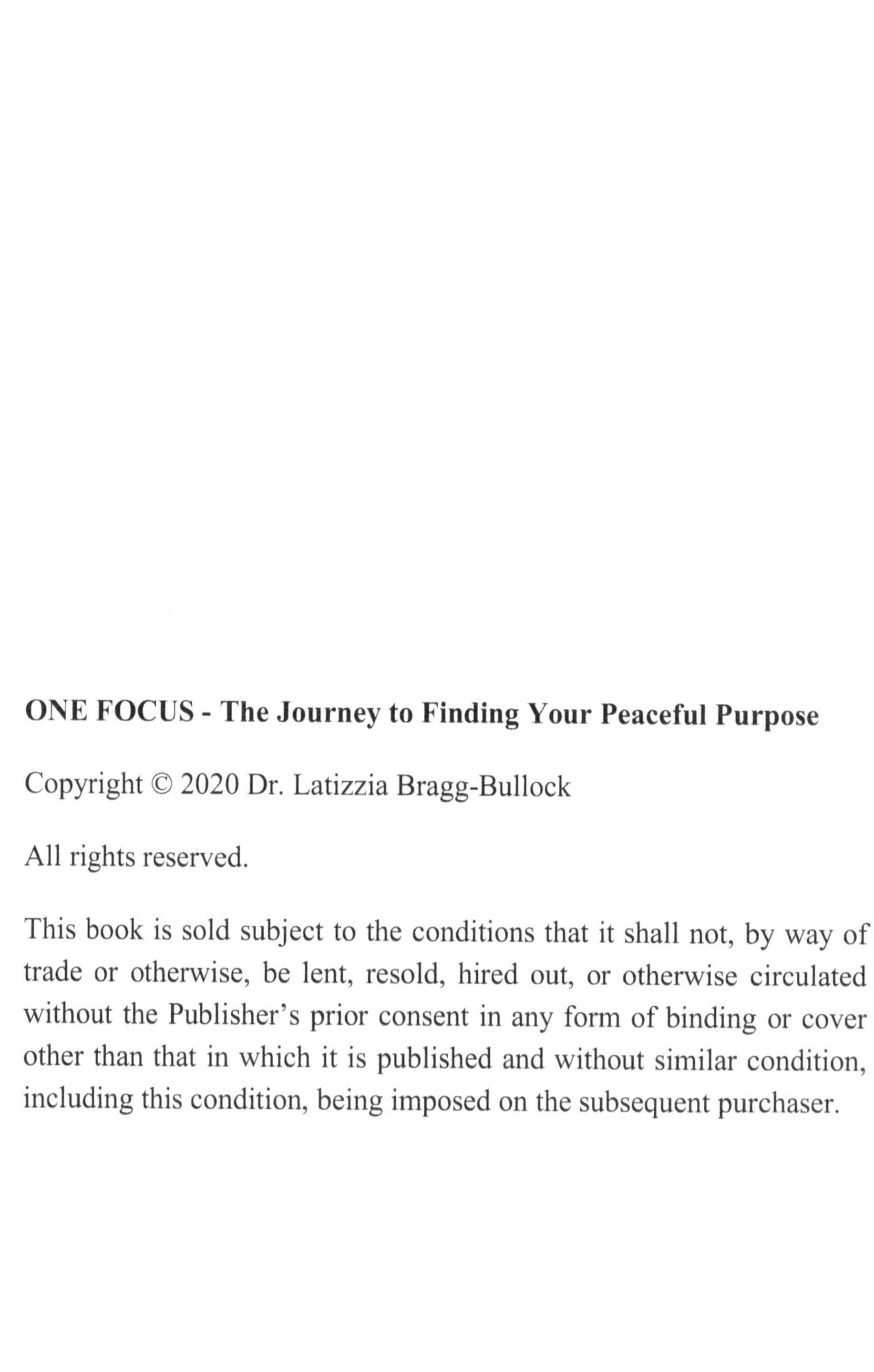

ONE FOCUS - The Journey to Finding Your Peaceful Purpose

Copyright © 2020 Dr. Latizzia Bragg-Bullock

This book is sold subject to the conditions that it shall not, by way of trade or otherwise, be lent, resold, hired out, or otherwise circulated without the Publisher's prior consent in any form of binding or cover other than that in which it is published and without similar condition, including this condition, being imposed on the subsequent purchaser.

This book is in loving memory of my mom
Betty L. Bragg
An example of love

Contents

THE JOURNEY

ACKNOWLEDGEMENTS

To my Heavenly Father for giving me this gift. I am truly grateful for your word, which has given me the encouragement to pursue my purpose.

To my son, King Trey, I am grateful for your giving spirit and the intelligent man you have become. You are such an inspiration.

To my daughter, Princess Nia, for your words of encouragement and sense of style I admire. You are truly my little fashionista.

To my mother for her unconditional love, support and words of encouragement.

To my father for your support and encouragement to read; it has truly been a gift.

To my pastor, Rev. Lance Watson, for over two decades of encouragement. Thank you for continuously feeding my spirit.

INTRODUCTION
Becoming Empowered

One Focus: The Journey to Finding Your Peaceful Purpose is an empowerment program designed to help demonstrate how to find one's life purpose. It is a unique autobiography. It details my life experiences that propelled me to seek my peaceful purpose. It serves as a tool to heal, empower and teach others **how to discover** their peaceful purpose as well as **how to maintain** while walking in one's calling. It teaches life skills that foster inner peace, joy and confidence, which most of us are seeking. The information shared in this book details the journey to discovering one's journey, therefore it provides a transparent description of the peaks as well as valleys that are inevitable and essential parts of our purposeful journey. In essence, it provides inspirational information and personal stories to help others successfully transition through the gains and losses we experience along the way as we seek our meaningful purpose filled with abundant joy, peace and prosperity.

Throughout the journey, we need to be mindful that our biggest hindrance is fear—*f*alse *e*vidence that *a*ppears *r*eal—because it only serves to hinder our journey to fulfilling our vision/mission. Thus, *One Focus: The Journey to Finding Your Peaceful Purpose* emphasizes spiritual and emotional healing. Consequently, having a peaceful existence requires emotional balance, which will result in joy or calm delight. Because we are considered the busiest generation ever in history, it is critical for us to utilize tools such as this program to maintain inner peace and balance in the midst of so much chaos. It is my belief that life is simply a learning school, and what you learn and give (teach) determines your experiences of fulfillment and balance. I'll use real life experiences to serve as examples of how I achieved a holistic balance, which created my peaceful existence. The term *holistic* is used throughout the book to describe the mental, physical, social, emotional and spiritual areas of one's life.

In *One Focus,* I share my life experiences growing from a child into a mature empowered woman to inspire and improve the lives of women. Often, women are caretakers, nurturers and the cohesive backbones of the family unit. Therefore, I believe that if we empower the women, we will ultimately empower the entire family, community and nation. My story includes the vicious cycle of ups and downs, and battles that I experienced personally and professionally, which help me achieve the victory of inner peace. I discovered that life is cyclical and transitional, and it should be embraced as a new lesson waiting to be learned. I realized that God created cycles of ups and downs for all beings—even for the waves in the ocean and the leaves in the fall. Therefore, it is natural that we, too, experience periods of ups and downs. My cycle consisted primarily of periods of favor and rejection. I experienced rejection or persecution from family, friends and professional acquaintances. Initially, I felt emotional pain and sadness; however, instead of remaining depressed and angry, I learned to simply detach, knowing that others behaviors are a result of their life experiences, to look for the lesson and to examine myself to see how I may have contributed to the experience.

In *One Focus*, the journey to discovering one's purpose consists of six major sections: **Discovery Lane** - *Discovering Your Peaceful Purpose*, **Adversity Turnpike** - *Grieving the Sunset*, **Positivity Boulevard** - *Midday: Surviving Through Purpose*, **Sunshine Parkway** - *Sunrise: Healing Through Purpose*, **Relationships Highway** - *Legacy of Light* and **Purpose Road** - *Walking in Your Miraculous, Noble Purpose*. **Discovery Lane** details my transitional childhood and young adult experiences, educational pursuits and love relationships. It provides skills for managing life transitions with inner peace, joy and confidence. **Adversity Turnpike** details my mid-life experiences with surviving loss; however, the life skills shared can be utilized when experiencing loss of any kind; for example, loss of one's job, income, position, etc. The different stages of grieving are detailed as well. This section of the book empowers and provides life skills to help others transition through the grieving process with inner peace and wholeness. The section entitled **Positivity Boulevard** details the positive emotions we will experience after we transition through the loss grieving process. The section entitled **Sunshine Parkway** details the process of healing, which is essential to the full manifestation of one's purpose. This section provides stress management skills needed to persevere through the inherent losses and periods of grief that accompany living a life of purpose. The section entitled **Relationships Highway** provides peaceful marriage, life purpose and parenting skills based on my real-life experiences. Each of the life skills learned will foster peaceful and powerful families in the 21st century and beyond. Lastly, the **Purpose Road** section details the lessons learned and the miracles witnessed along the path to discovering and walking in my purpose. It is an insightful and inspirational account of my personal experiences. It provides insight on how to persevere once you have discovered your life's purpose. In essence, *One Focus* means having our focus on spirit because it is this focus that sustains and propels us forward in the midst of life transitions and adversities.

I suggest that you keep a pen or pencil near so that you can complete the "Reflection Exercises" at the end of each chapter. Please complete the exercises in their entirety. They were designed to give you greater insight into your peaceful purpose. Ultimately, walking in love creates a transformation that will reveal your peaceful purpose and result in harmonious interactions with others, your family, friends and coworkers. You will be able to transition through your life's journey with inner peace, joy and confidence, whether you are grieving a loss or celebrating a gain. Be mindful that balance should be our aim.

I sought many "holistic" sources for answers to my life's ups and downs. In other words, I often asked myself, *what is life really about? Why am I here? What is my life's assignment or purpose?* Consequently, I learned even joyous occasions or transitions; for example, marriage or the birth of a child, can diminish or heighten our inner peace. For answers to my purpose, I sought religious spiritual group activity, such as regular church attendance for answers (spiritual). Secondly, I sought acquisition of the world's knowledge by obtaining a Bachelors, Masters, Post-Masters Certificate and Doctorate for answers (mental). Third, I sought exercise for answers (physical) and, finally, I sought self help books for answers (emotional and social). After all of that searching, I returned to my spiritual quest and sought an individual relationship with spirit through reading the Bible and discovered the answer! Within the pages of the Bible I discovered the spiritual, emotional, mental, physical and social answers I needed to realize my life's purpose. I overcame transitions often disguised as problems and adversities, and I grew. Instinctively, I would turn my focus to God in the midst of my life's trials, and ultimately received the very thing I prayed for and more. I really did not clearly see the connection until much later because hindsight is 20/20 vision. It is my belief that the ability to make connections is a divine gift.

I realized that keeping "one focus" was helping me to persevere and achieve my God-given vision, which was my life purpose. I believe now I am empowered to help others improve their lives and overcome life transitions and negative adverse cycles. Being a "peaceful being" was my life's desire and now I know the way to it. We have to cultivate a lifestyle of peace. We should seek peace every day in every situation. Peace cannot exist without an act of love. Therefore, we should seek to love others and ourselves as well as our life experiences whether they are good, bad or growth-provoking. If we seek to improve the lives of others by giving love, peace will reign in our lives. In essence, our ability to walk in love through life's transitions will result in inner peace. Thus, I realized that I could not remain in a peaceful state of mind in the world by myself; it was only possible with God. "I can do all things through Christ who strengthens me" (Philippians 4:13). I matured and learned to enjoy my purposeful work of improving the lives of others by sharing inspirational, transparent information via dialogue, books, mentoring and educational venues, workshops, seminars as well as business, marketing and life skills courses. As a result, abundant fruits of the spirit manifested; for example, the love of giving others joy, peace, patience, kindness, goodness, gentleness, faith, modesty, chastity and self-control. Finally, my search for life's answers to inner peace was over, (and yours too). I learned that staying focused on spirit through regular spiritual connection, attending church, reflective journaling and reading God's word resulted in the organic manifestation of my life's purpose. In essence, I realized that Love=Peace and God's word-spirit must be our focus so we can truly walk in our vision/mission.

Discovery Lane

~Discovering Your Peaceful Purpose~

This section details my journey from childhood to adulthood. It illustrates empowerment—the power to make decisions independently. In this section you will see how your purpose is revealed through your different life stages and experiences. Focusing on hope, good (positives) and truth propelled me to persevere and seek my peaceful purpose.

1

Seed of Purpose

Love always Hopes

Today's working definition of **Hope:**

This peace-provoking act requires us to have positive expectations, regardless of current conditions or circumstances. Remember that hope is one of the greatest gifts' life has to offer.

What is one's life purpose? Our purpose is a life-long desire or dream that we hunger for deep inside of our heart and mind. Our past gives clues to our purpose.

So, my journey of hope begins…

In 1964, I was born in Virginia. My dad was a 21-year-old college student and my mom was a 17-year-old high school student. My mom's older sister introduced them. I was born shortly thereafter. Later, they got married because it was the honorable thing to do in the 1960's. My dad was the middle of three children and his mother was an early widowed schoolteacher who resided in the south. My mom was raised as the baby girl by her step-grandmother and was later placed in foster homes. Although both of my parents had uncommon backgrounds, they had common attraction for each other. Despite my dad's background—fatherless at a young age—he was authoritative, ambitious and hardworking because he assumed the paternal role of helping his mother with his two siblings. Also, because his mom was a teacher, he developed a love for reading, which I inherited. I strongly feel that my love for reading is the greatest gift I received from my dad. Because my mom was the baby girl, she was shy and spoiled, but extremely encouraging. Later, I realized that my desire to encourage others is the greatest gift my mom has given me. As a result, I wrote this book to encourage others. Do you see the connection? We are truly a result of our upbringing.

My parents' marriage lasted approximately five years. They experienced the typical ups and downs, but they were young and in love. As a result of their separation due to my dad's infidelity, my mom and I moved to Washington DC. We lived there for seven years, which is the number of completions. God completed creating heaven and earth and everything in it by the seventh day. My mom was overwhelmed with the pressure of trying to raise a child as a single parent without spiritual connection and a tenth-grade education. My mom dropped out of high school due to her pregnancy with me.

Later, she became pregnant again with my brother, and she applied for Welfare, which is temporary government financial assistance for needy families. We moved back to Virginia and sought housing with her oldest sister. That environment, along with the financial pressure, caused my mom more emotional distress. As a result, she became more overwhelmed, depressed and needed medical attention. Thus, her younger sister called the police and the city officer placed my infant brother and myself in a foster home. Much later, I realized that low self-esteem is the result of having a prolonged pity party with self. I also discovered that there was a direct correlation between depression and one's self-esteem or self-perception. Consequently, if we do not have a spiritual foundation to know that we are special to God and that our lives are purposeful, our self-esteem as we journey through life will, oftentimes, be diminished.

While I was in the foster home, my dad was contacted to assume custody of me. I lived with him and his new wife, whose sense of style I admire. I lived with them for a short time before I was shifted to live with my paternal grandmother, the schoolteacher. This adjustment was difficult for me because I missed my mother deeply. Although my grandmother loved me and tried to ease my transition with an abundance of gifts and beautiful clothes, she could not compensate for the pain in my heart due to the separation from my mom, who I love and adored beyond measure. I only stayed there for one school year due to my unhappiness. I was then sent by my dad to live with his sister, who I now view as an excellent role model. She worked full-time as an elementary school teacher like her mom, dutiful wife and mother. In high school, I was called to the guidance office because they could not locate my school records. By the time I reached high school, I had attended fourteen different schools. Throughout all the transition I experienced in my childhood, my mother's love was my foundation for hope.

I share my childhood to demonstrate all the transition I experienced. I believe my mom had unconditional love for me, and my hope for a brighter tomorrow helped me endure and find inner peace in the midst of all the change. The key is simply to stay focused on the love in your life and hope for a better tomorrow. Don't focus on the change; focus on the positive outcome. Hold on to love and you will have hope in addition to peace in the midst of transition. Consequently, my mom's favorite song was "Our Day Will Come". Mine has and so will yours.

~Fruits of Peace~

Your Assigned Peaceful Purpose Formula

Your Life Experience

Your Education/Training

<u>Your Abilities</u>

Your Assigned Peaceful Purpose

In my workshop entitled "Walking in the Light of Your Purpose," one of the participants who was contemplating a career transition shared with me that my presentation was "powerful." Also, she stated, "I found myself taking notes throughout and was absorbed by the truth that was shared." So, get your pen and paper ready to discover how to find and walk into your purpose.

Remember, our purpose manifests when we realize our true inner divinity by focusing on spirit and our connection to the Higher Power. Ultimately, our purpose is the key to unlocking the door of prosperity and abundance.

Reflection Exercise

Love Always Hopes

The Power of Words:

I. Speak Positives - My Affirmation Statement:

Say it aloud and write the affirmation statement 7 times.

*Remember, 7 symbolizes completion.

"I am a loving and hopeful being."

II. Serve Self and Others - My Love Walk:

Love always creates inner peace!

Today, I walked in love by hoping for or expecting a positive outcome to _______________________. (Give your personal example.)

III. Relax - Silent Moments of Connection:

Circle or write a peaceful action you practiced today.

*Remember, guarding our mouths creates inner peace. *

- ❖ No gossiping
- ❖ No complaining
- ❖ No blaming

Create moments of silence *light a candle*

❖ No TV

❖ No music

❖ No cell phone

❖ No Internet/No Social Media

IV. Be Grateful - Gratitude Journal Entry: Fill in the blank.

"Today, I am thankful for ________________."

2
The Season of Maturity

Love Delights in Good

Today's working definition: **Good** means doing the right thing.

This inner-peace-provoking act requires us to first know what is right and the consequences of our choices. It requires us to do what is right unconditionally, no matter what. In essence, it demands decision-making skills based on honesty and integrity.

Our natural qualities and past experiences give us *clues* to our purpose. Also, our physical design and packaging is well-suited for our purpose.

So, the journey to good begins…

Upon graduating from high school, I desired to get baptized. I began reading the Bible prior to going to college. Immediately following my high school graduation, I went to live with my mom. However, approaching graduation, I started experiencing severe migraine headaches due to stress, per my doctor's evaluation. Therefore, I did not attend my pre-graduation ceremony. The stress came from fear because I was constantly reminded that, once I turned 18 years old, I would be on my own, and knowing my mom's financial situation, I became fearful. Despite this, I went to live with her. I loved my mom and had deep compassion for her, and I did not want to add another financial burden on her while I saved money for college. However, she was all I had. I continued to apply to different colleges in the north. My two best friends in high school planned to go up north to college too. I was excited about being accepted to Morgan State University (MSU) in Baltimore, Maryland, but I was fearful due to the distance and the change. The Sunday prior to going off to college, my father and I attend church. Occasionally, my dad would take me to church, which I later appreciated a great deal. Following the church service, my dad had a heart attack. Consequently, I decided not to attend MSU because of the distance and my father's condition. I felt that he needed me because I was his only child. Ironically, throughout my upbringing with my father, I would often say, "One day he is going to need me." This is when I began to realize the power of words. "Guard thy tongue, He who holds his tongue is wise" (Proverbs 10:19). I believe that my dad's main concern was working, like most men. This was apparent by his decisions to send me to live with his various relatives. Since I decided not to attend MSU, I worked full-time and attended a community college at home to save money and buy a car.

I worked hard with long hours in retail sales and was promoted to the Head of Sales position. I really enjoyed this position because of the added responsibility and the opportunity to save more money for college. Once I had saved enough money, I enrolled in a four-year university in Norfolk, Virginia. I overcame my fear of being away from my family, and I established a true sense of independence. I was tapping into the power within—an act of empowerment. I attended the university in Norfolk, Virginia for two years. Throughout college, I attended church regularly, which helped to encourage me to endure the financial hardships, unfair treatment and other trials. I gained my independence and became self-supporting. However, the financial hardships I experienced in school began to take a toll. Oftentimes, I would pray for a job so I could stay in school and pay my $100 car note. I loved school because I believed it gave me hope for a brighter tomorrow; however, the financial stress became overwhelming. In the midst of it all, my prayers were soon answered, and I got two jobs—one in retail sales and the other through a government funded stay-in-school program. Ironically, the government job was the beginning of my career in health claims.

On a daily basis, I communicated with people who were hurting. Now my struggle involved trying to maintain two part-time jobs while attending college full-time. I decided to transfer back home to attend college to lighten my financial burden. One of my high school friends had also transferred back home from college in Maryland and she told me about a college transfer grant. I prayed, preserved and held onto the hope of a brighter future. As a result, I reached my goal: I received my bachelor's degree from Virginia Commonwealth University in 1985. I thought my struggles were over.

Being a product of a family of educators, I was always told that education was a good thing. Therefore, I wanted to do those things that would ensure a brighter tomorrow for my future family and myself. Although I experienced financial hardships as I prayed and turned to God, (focused on spirit) I was able to persevere and maintain inner peace. Therefore, I encourage you to seek what is good, always pray and keep pressing on. Your answer will manifest. That, I promise. More importantly, God promised!

Reflection Exercise

Love Delights in Good

The Power of Words:

I. Speak Positives - My Affirmation Statement:

Say aloud and write the affirmation statement 7 times.

"I am prospering because I delight in doing good."

II. Serve Self and Others - My Love Walk

Love always creates inner peace!

Today, I walked in love by demonstrating an act of goodness to my friends, family members, coworkers, customers, etc.

III. Relax - Silent Moments of Connection:

Circle or write a peaceful action you practiced today.

*Remember, guarding our mouths creates inner peace.

❖ No gossiping

❖ No complaining

❖ No blaming

Create moments of silence *light a candle*

- ❖ No TV
- ❖ No music
- ❖ No cell phone
- ❖ No Internet/No Social Media

IV. Be Grateful - Gratitude Journal Entry: Fill in the blank.
"Today, I am thankful for _________________."

3
The Fall Changes

Love Rejoices in the Truth

Today's working definition: **Truth** means being honest and not pretentious.

This inner-peace-provoking act requires honesty with oneself and others. First, we must examine ourselves and be true to ourselves before we can be true to others. Having character based on integrity is critical to your purposeful leadership position. We should not compromise the value of truth and honesty for anything or anyone.

Pursuing our spiritual truth manifests our purpose, which liberates or frees us from oppressive jobs and relationships.

So, my journey to truth begins…

I soon discovered that close relationships provide a mirror of our soul so we can learn about ourselves, as well as our likes and dislikes. I was what they call a "late bloomer" in comparison to my peers in the 80's. My first date was my prom date, who also became my first boyfriend. Because I lacked experience in dating, I did not know how to respond in certain situations, but I soon learned. I quickly realized the traits I did not like and the ones I did like in men and myself. The most important one was being honest and truthful. It was my experience that the truth always manifests when we least expect it. The attributes that I did not like consisted of the following: being pretentious, untruthful, selfish or controlling, to name a few. Attributes I later appreciated were caring, giving, stimulating conversation and athletic hobbies. I had matured in this area without being aware of it. During those days, the way someone looked was the important decision-making factor when it came to partner selection. As I matured, I began to realize that the outward packaging is OK, but the inner substance, a man's heart (feelings) and mind (faith) were by far the most important factors.

Although I had an off and on relationship for over a decade with the same man, I could see a pattern or vicious cycle. I realized that many men were immature, pretentious and simply self-seeking. Consequently, during this time in my life it seemed whenever I would attend church service, the sermon topic was fornication, which I believe made me more conscious of the pattern. I began to feel convicted. As a result, most of my young, single adult period was without male companionship. Oftentimes, I would partake in physical activities (hobbies) such as jogging, aerobics and biking. My primary passion was running, I would often go to the park or a high school track and run for hours. The release of endorphins, the chemical hormone release in the brain when exercising, always seemed to make me feel much better and forget my loneliness. I came to realize that we are all a mixed bag with some good and bad attributes. The question becomes, *what are you willing to accept? Do the good attributes outweigh the bad? What are the most important attributes to you?* I simply began to look for the gift in each relationship as well as the lesson learned. Do realize that life's lessons are a gift? Here are some of the gifts I received from my relationships: the ability to love and forgive unconditionally, an appreciation for truthfulness, giving, a sense of humor and a love for jazz music. Also, I learned how to play tennis and ski. I believe everything I experienced was good. I encourage you to look for the gift that each relationship brings as well as the lessons received.

~Fruits of Peace~

One Focus Stages

<u>Focus</u>	<u>Ages</u>
Relationship	**20**
Educational	**20-25**
Emotional/Experiences	**25-35**
Power	**35-40**
Legacy	**40+**

***This is likely where you are if you are reading this book because,**
in this stage, you are perfecting your purpose/calling.
All of life experiences come together.
One begins to reach the place of their greatest accomplishments.
One Focus is POWER!

Remember, the lesson is often the gift. Get off the vicious turbulent waves and cruise through life's journey with a faithful purpose. Remember, we have the power within each of us, and how we respond determines our experiences. Also, the truth is the light, and pure, unconditional love finds inner peace by focusing on the spirit and joy that resides in living in your truth.

Reflection Exercise

Love Rejoices in the Truth

The Power of Words:

I. Speak Positives - My Affirmation Statement:

Say it aloud and write the affirmation statement 7 times.

"I am experiencing joy because I am continually rejoicing in God's truth."

II. Serve Self and Others - My Love Walk:

Love always creates inner peace!

Today, I walked in love by keeping promises, i.e. being true to family members, friends, coworkers, etc. (Give your personal example.)

III. Relax/Meditate - Silent Moments of Connection:

Circle or write a peaceful action you practiced today.

*Remember, guarding our mouths creates inner peace.

- ❖ No gossiping
- ❖ No complaining
- ❖ No blaming

Create moments of silence *light a candle*

- ❖ No TV
- ❖ No music
- ❖ No cell phone
- ❖ No Internet/No Social Media

IV. Be Grateful - Gratitude Journal Entry: Fill in the blank. "Today, I am thankful for _________________."

Adversity Turnpike

~Grieving the Sunset~

*This section gives a brief synopsis of my mom's terminal illness and death. Although it details my intense mid-life experience with grief due to the loss of a loved one, the skills provided in this section can be applied to loss of any kind, for example, loss of a job, income, peace, joy, etc. It provides life skills and stress management techniques to help others move through the grieving process successfully with inner peace and healing-wholeness. We will experience losses as well as triumphs along our journey to discovering and walking in our purpose, this section details our common responses to loss and how to get to the other side of the valley or loss so we can live an abundant life of purpose. The Sunset focuses on **Giving**, the foundational cornerstone for unconditional love.*

4
Sunset's Twilight Spring

Love is Giving

Today's working definition: **Giving** means unconditional sharing.

This inner-peace-provoking act requires us to sacrifice some part of ourselves. It is the foundation of unconditional love.

The greatest tragedy in life is not death but living a life without meaning or purpose.

So, my journey of giving begins…

It was April. The flowers were beginning to bloom, and the birds were returning. The weather was wonderful. However, all was unnoticed by my mother and me. My mom had been experiencing stomach pain due to gastric difficulties and was undergoing many diagnostic procedures to determine the cause. Initially, she was diagnosed with a defective gallbladder, which was removed because she had developed jaundice. Then, she was diagnosed with complications of the bile duct, which was restructured. However, she continued to experience stomach pain and gastric problems. As a result, she sought additional diagnostic tests. The test revealed abnormalities in my mom's pancreas and liver. She underwent a biopsy and, again, awaited the results. The results stated that she had the "Big C" –cancer of the pancreas—as well as spots on her liver. We went to see an oncologist for further information about this horrifying diagnosis. I wanted my mom to receive a course of treatment to sustain her life. Working in healthcare, I was somewhat knowledgeable about medical diagnoses and procedures. After we met with the internist, we left his office sad, irritated and confused as to why the doctors did not see these symptoms earlier. In the car ride home, we shared our frustrations and feelings. I drove my mom home and I could not wait to get to my apartment to really release what I was truly feeling. I did not want her to know my fear because I did not want her to worry; I knew I had to be strong for her. When I returned to my apartment, I screamed and cried out to God. I did not want my mother to see how I was really feeling. Later, my mom called, and we talked more about the early evening happenings. I comforted my mom and told her everything was going to be OK, and that I was going to contact that oncologist the internist had referred and inquire about a plan of treatment. I called and made an appointment for my mom with the oncologist. I asked him not to discuss the prognosis in front of my mom because of her history of depression. I did not want her to worry. I tried to be a trooper for my mom.

The oncologist called me into the office and advised me of my mom's dim prognosis. He stated that she only had three months to live, and the only thing he could offer for treatment of pancreatic/liver cancer were pain pills to help relieve her stomach pain and discomfort. I refused to believe this terrible prognosis. I simply held onto hope, believing that God was sovereign. I inquired about chemotherapy as a means of saving or prolonging my mom's life. He stated that the use of chemotherapy with his kind of cancer was not successful, but if I wanted my mom to undergo it, he would administer an aggressive protocol of chemotherapy consistent with young age. I thought I had to do whatever I could to help prolong my mom's life. This included a lot of prayer, chemotherapy and natural health cues. I searched for an inkling of hope rather than simply administering pain pills and waiting for her to die. My mom underwent the chemotherapy successfully. Every day of her 5-day chemotherapy protocol, I was concerned about the side effects, which I had read about, but my mom was a real trooper.

After she was released from the hospital, I continued to read literature on pancreatic and liver cancer and went to the health food store to buy vitamins, Aloe Vera juice, ginseng drinks and whatever else I could find. I was trying to help rebuild her immune system after the protocol of chemotherapy. As my mom continued to recover, I cooked her nutritious meals with beets, spinach, cauliflower, etc. Although my mom lost her appetite, I strongly encouraged her to continue eating to rebuild her body. My mom stayed with me for a couple of days but was anxious to return home. Reluctantly, I took her home and tried not to take her desire to return home personally. However, I had become very protective over her.

My mom was fine for a while, but as the weeks progressed, the side effects that I had read about started to manifest. Dealing with her own mortality, my mom slipped into a depression, which was one of the side effects of chemotherapy due to the chemical imbalance. She started mentally revisiting all the negative experiences she had encountered throughout the course of her life. She was beginning to grieve. I reluctantly listened and encouraged her to pray and think positive. "God will pull us through," I shared. During my mom's grieving process, she became resentful and hostile towards the doctors. I took off from work to take her for chemotherapy follow-up visits with the oncologist. One time she walked out of the office fearful and angry. This really upset me because I too was fearful, but I was trying to do everything I could to help prolong my mom's life. At this point, she was not cooperating. When I would take my mom home and I was alone in my apartment, I would cry. I was brokenhearted, and I felt hopeless. My mom called and, this time, I could not mask my true feelings. I began to cry uncontrollably and blurted out, "I don't want you to die. You are not only my mom; you are my sister I never had and my best friend." I continued to encourage her to press on and cooperate with the doctors. I continued to buy nutritious groceries for her meals and encouraged her to return to church, but my mom only wanted to reflect on her cancer. I brought her crafts to keep her mind occupied during the day, but she continued to slip into depression. She began cleaning her house, anticipating her death. She called me to get all her meaningful belongings because she wanted me to have them when she died. My mom's dialogue and actions devastated me. I too underwent a great deal of emotional anxiety, but I continued to pray, persevere and encourage my mom to have hope.

My mom was heavy-laden, dealing with her own mortality, and continued to regress into a deep depression. She later had an accident and her house caught on fire. Due to my mom's depression, the officials considered her actions a suicide attempt and she was treated accordingly. I rushed from work to be by my mom's side. She stayed in the hospital under medical observation. Finally, the doctors transferred my mom to another hospital where she underwent treatment for depression. Consequently, while she was in the hospital, I contacted our pastor and he made a personal visit to the hospital. When she was released, I picked her up and we went to dinner, shopping and to the hair salon. I hoped these actions would pick up her spirits. I also promised her a trip. We went to get the bus tickets for her to visit with relatives up north. My mom stated she had a very nice time. Afterward, I brought thank-you cards for the relatives my mom visited and the pastor. There was peace again. I continued to monitor my mom's diet and properly administer her medications. She appeared to be doing somewhat OK; however, the cancer had begun to spread to her brain. This was the beginning of the very end. Her ability to walk and talk was impaired. She could not sit up or complete a sentence. Every day I came to the hospital to visit her, she would moan, sing and sleep. She passed on August 16, 1994, peacefully in her sleep at the young age of forty-seven. I prepared and carried out the funeral arrangements. It was truly a beautiful homegoing celebration for the most giving, encouraging and loving mother anyone could have asked for. On the other hand, this was the most painful experience for me, and it got worse after things settled down and the reality of never being able to talk to my mom again overwhelmed me with grief. I was truly heart broken. For weeks, if not months, I wept and cried out to the Lord, because I felt fear, loneliness and emptiness. I was in the depression stage of grieving. I even thought of committing suicide because the one person I loved more than anyone was gone. Unfortunately, suicide is very common in this country; approximately 30,000 Americans take their lives annually. There are more suicides than murders. My loss was unbearable, but with prayer, I persevered. Thus, a new and wonderful beginning awaited me. I know what it is like to lose a loved one, so I encourage you to give God what belongs to him and he will reward you. You will not be left alone. Just hold on!

Remember that you can get through transitions with inner peace and a sound mind only by being connected to God. Therefore, I encourage you to stay connected to your power source. Faith in God will give you the strength to endure and so much more. God truly understands what it means to give or sacrifice a loved one. After all, he gave his only begotten son, Jesus Christ!

I know you are thinking, *good grief, what a lot of grief!* I believe I had to go through this intense pain of loss to help others through the darkness of loss to the path of light while maintaining inner peace, love and a sound mind. We cannot help someone else heal from pain until we have the personal experience ourselves. Experience is life's best teacher.

In the next chapters, we will explore the stages of dealing with loss. Survivors experience four negative emotions: denial, anger, blame and depression. These emotions are natural when dealing with loss of any kind. Be patient with yourself and remember that grief is a mental struggle. Our goal is to mentally train ourselves to focus on our healing and not our loss.

Reflection Exercise

Love is Giving

The Power of Words:

I. Speak Positives - My Affirmation Statement:

Say it aloud and write the affirmation statement 7 times.

"I am abundantly and unconditionally giving everywhere I go."

II. Serve Self and Others - My Love Walk:

Love always creates inner peace!

Today, I walked in love by giving without expecting anything in return from family, friends, coworkers, clients, etc. (Give your personal example.)

III. Relax/Meditate - Silent Moments of Connection:

Circle or write a peaceful action you practiced today.

*Remember, guarding our mouths creates inner peace.

- ❖ No gossiping
- ❖ No complaining
- ❖ No blaming

Create moments of silence *light a candle

- ❖ No TV
- ❖ No music
- ❖ No cell phone
- ❖ No Internet/No Social Media

IV. Be Grateful - Gratitude Journal Entry: Fill in the blank. "Today, I am thankful for ________________."

5
Sunset's Denial

"The truth shall set you free"
(John 8:32)

Denial is a natural negative emotion that is often part of the grieving process. When in denial, we don't want to accept the truth of the lost loved one, job, income, etc. In the case of receiving news of a terminal illness, grieving due to fear once the news is received. Thus, the grieving process can begin prior to the actual death of a loved one. Although **"FEAR"** is (F) false (E) evidence that (A) appears (R) real, it can often produce emotions about the reality prior to the actual loss. As I mentioned earlier, these negative emotions can occur when experiencing any kind of loss in one's life. Consequently, dealing with adversity or loss often interferes with our inner peace. When we experience denial, we have a tendency to not believe the sad news that we have received because it is too painful and we may have a pinch of hope lingering in our hearts that the death will or has not occurred. In denial, we think there has been some mistake. We believe this should not have happened to us. We have a tendency to take the death personally. Often, because the loved one is close to us, their pain becomes our pain. We question ourselves, "What have I done to deserve this?" We often review and analyze our lives, searching for errors that could explain the loss. Consequently, when our loved ones die, part of the survivor dies also.

I'll never forget when my mom called me from the hospital after she received the results from the biopsy that revealed she had cancer. I was at work and I was trying to mentally process the horrifying news. I immediately thought this could not be true. I was in a state of denial, and I did not want to believe the diagnosis because it was too painful. Thankfully, it was at the end of my workday because I was overwhelmed by the news of the cancer diagnosis. After I got home, I cried. The cancer had become real to me. The denial was over. I would often pray for strength to persevere. Remember, people who achieve greatness are realistic. Therefore, seek the truth. Do not live in denial.

Reflection Exercise
Denial

The Power of Words:

I. Speak Positives - My Affirmation Statement:

Say it aloud and write the affirmation statement 7 times.

"I am accepting the truth in all situations."

II. Serve Others - My Love Walk:

Love always creates inner peace!

Today, I demonstrated love by accepting the reality of my loss by continuing to maintain close relationships with other loved ones. (Give your personal example.)

III. Relax/Meditate - Silent Moments of Connection:

My example:

Turn off the TV, cell phone, etc. Take 10 minutes of "quiet time" to engage in inner dialogue and validate your feelings of denial. Remember, it is natural for survivors to initially experience denial.

IV. Be Grateful - Gratitude Journal Entry: Fill in the blank.
"Today, I am thankful for ___________________"

6
Sunset's Anger

"In your anger do not sin"
(Ephesians 4:26)

nger is often the second negative emotion survivors experience when faced with the death of a loved one, job, income, etc. Its purpose is to warn us that something is wrong. Therefore, it is OK to get angry, but it is our negative reaction that can be detrimental. Anger is a fear-based emotion. Fear is the enemy of peaceful healing. It is impossible to heal with negative, fearful thoughts. We can only heal when we program our mind to allow positive thoughts to overshadow the negative thoughts. Although anger is a natural emotion involving death or loss of any kind, we can choose not to be led by it. We simply cannot allow ourselves to respond negatively or exhibit any negative behavior, although we may want to lash out at others when we are angry and in pain. This is due to our natural tendency to react to a negative stimulus in a negative way. As children we are conditioned to group like items, but as we mature, we must be mindful that this rule of grouping does not apply to negative behavior. There are always exceptions to every general rule, and this is the exception. Only positive behavior should be paired with negative behavior in order for us to be successful in social interactions.

If we choose to react negatively out of anger, it may result in self-inflicted injury or injury to others. We need to be conscious of the fact that anger is inner pain that manifests itself outwardly in abusive ways. It is often revealed as excessive negative behavior. Consequently, this pain-generated anger can be inflicted on others, or ourselves. When it is inflicted on us, it can be in the form of substance abuse, promiscuity, or excessive worrying. However, if it is inflicted on others, it may be demonstrated as mental abuse or physical abuse. In mentally abusive situations, the angry person attempts to hurt others by using negative words with a lot of name-calling, blaming, false accusations and cursing. In physically abusive situations, the angry individual hurts others by the negative use of personal power. This is often viewed as violent behavior. Consequently, if the anger is not managed, it can be harmful and damaging to self and others, mentally as well as physically. Often, the angry person's misuse of personal power results in damaged relationships with self and others. In essence, anger has a negative effect on how we think about ourselves as well as how others think about us. We should choose to use our personal power in a positive way so that we don't suffer mental pain from regret in addition to the loss. Therefore, we need to choose to be peaceful, not harmful. Keep in mind, it is often the people who are hurting who hurt others. Don't take the angry, abusive behavior directed toward you personally. Remember, there is always more than what we can see. Also, their behavior reflects that person's life experience or lack of knowledge.

I also experienced this stage when I was grieving. I began to feel angry about my mom's diagnosis. We were in the car returning from the initial visit with the internist who discovered the cancer. He had shown us the x-rays and the computer graphics that revealed the location of the cancer on the liver and pancreas. Following this, my mom and I began to share our anger with the doctor simply because he was the source of the negative information. I had to remind myself that he did not put the cancer inside of my mom, but, due to overwhelming negative, fear-based emotions, I was sometimes unable to intellectualize the situation.

In my "Anger Management" workshop, I encouraged the participants not to take the "bait" by responding to a negative behavior in the same manner and reward themselves with self-love and pampering activities when they are successful. Sheri, one of the participants, stated she would not give her power away and will choose a proactive, incompatible response. Also, I like the idea of rewarding herself, and she looked forward to her rewards. Remember, anger serves as a warning that something is wrong. Take heed and proceed with peaceful care.

Reflection Exercise

Anger

The Power of Words:

I. Speak Positives - My Affirmation Statement:

Say it aloud and write the affirmation statement 7 times.

"I am responding in love, not anger."

II. Serve Others - My Love Walk:

Love always creates inner peace!

Today, I demonstrated love by forgiving the doctors, my spouse, children, co-worker, etc. (Give your personal example.)

III. Relax/Meditate - Silent Moments of Connection:

Turn off the TV, cell phone etc.

Develop a "prayer" to specifically address your anger. Remember, anger is a strong emotion that should be controlled.

My prayer: ___________________."

IV. Be Grateful - Gratitude Journal Entry: Fill in the blank. "Today, I am thankful for ___________________."

7
Sunset's Blame

"Walk before me and be blameless."
(Genesis 17:1)

It is only natural to want to point the finger at someone else when we are grieving. However, we need to be aware that blaming others for our loss is immature, unfair, negative behavior. Blaming is simply complaining or sharing negative thoughts and feelings about our loss. We may have the tendency to blame ourselves as well as others. We think, *if only I had been there*. In maturity, we accept the fact that certain events in life are inevitable and required for our growth. Also, we cannot control others' actions. Mature survivors know they can only seek to serve as examples of peace with help from above.

Blaming or holding someone at fault always follows anger. Often, we blame others for our losses, loved ones, jobs, income, etc. Consequently, after I became angry about my mother's cancer, I immediately, unconsciously began to find someone to blame. Primarily, I blamed the doctor because she had been going to him for approximately two years complaining about stomach pain and gastric discomfort; however, he ordered no tests. It was not until she was taken to the emergency room for gastric problems that the emergency physician ordered her to return to the hospital for additional tests. It was the hospital test that discovered the cancer. Ultimately, I had to let go of my anger and blaming and seek acceptance by focusing on the high power at work, not the doctor. I realized that the act of blaming kept replaying the pain of the loss in my mind. I found peace in knowing that her suffering was over, although mine continued.

Remember, blaming is a negative emotion that simply increases our pain by mentally revisiting the negative memories pertaining to our loss. It only aids in focusing on the negative, so stop blaming and you will change your focus.

Reflection Exercise

Blame

The Power of Words:

I. Speak Positives - My Affirmation Statement:

Say it aloud and write the affirmation statement 7 times.

"I am not blaming myself or others for my loss"

II. Serve Self and Others - My Love Walk

Love always creates inner peace!

Today, I demonstrated love by not responding to my adversary's blame attack and by choosing to silently repeat an affirmation. (Give your personal example.)

III. Relax/Meditate - Silent Moments of Connection

Turn off the TV, cell phone, etc.

Reflect (or meditate) on the verse, "Be Blameless" (Psalm 119:1). What does this bible verse mean to you?

IV. Be Grateful - Gratitude Journal Entry: Fill in the blank. "Today, I am thankful for __________________."

8
Sunset's Depression

"Rejoice in our suffering because we know suffering produces perseverance, perseverance, character, and character hope."
(Romans 5:3, 4)

The fourth negative emotion survivors experience on their journey to peaceful healing after experiencing a loss of some kind is depression. In depression we are in a state of continuous sadness. Consequently, 20 million Americans suffer from depression and seek medication and counseling to deal with this mental agony. Often, we engage in self-pity. We simply have to choose whether we will be pitiful or powerful; the two cannot coexist. When we feel depressed or low in spirit, we are out of balance because of our conscious choice to focus on a loss or our deceased loved one. We must remember that fear is our enemy to inner healing, and it is only an illusion. Often, the very thing we fear most should not be feared at all. Everything in life is temporary. Having our mental power drained by negative emotions—denial, anger, and blame—causes depression.

In the grieving process, we should seek emotional stability. Consequently, we should be aware of our tendency to become manic-depressive. This is a psychological term used to describe people who go from one emotional extreme to another. In other words, the survivor is extremely happy (high) or extremely sad (low). We should choose to be emotionally well balanced or stable, whether we are experiencing a gain or a loss.

I was so busy during my mom's three months of illness with working full-time, attending graduate school part-time, managing both mine and my mom's homes, in addition to making a couple of trips to the hospital daily. Due to my busy schedule maintaining everything, I often did not have time to entertain negative thoughts of my mom's death. In addition, I was always hopeful that she would beat the cancer and it would go into remission. However, weeks after her funeral, I had more time to think about the finality of her death. As a result, my grieving became intense, and all the emotions were overwhelming. This was the beginning of my depression. I would often cry uncontrollably due to the heart-felt pain that resulted from my loss. To overcome depression, I had to change my focus from the negative (my mom's death) to the positive (my promising future). Also, I had to engage in holistic healing activities such as prayer and exercise.

Remember, depression focus is down, healing focus is up. Seek to be mentally and emotionally balanced, displaying calm and peaceful demeanor in all circumstances. Keep in mind, the pain of loss is only temporary, and a gain awaits you!

Reflection Exercise

Depression

The Power of Words:

I. Speak Positives - My Affirmation Statement:

Say it aloud and write the affirmation statement 7 times.

"I am focusing upward, therefore I do not allow my mind to entertain depressive, negative thoughts."

II. Serve Self and Others - My Love Walk:

Love always creates inner peace!

Today, I demonstrated love by identifying my depressive thoughts and emotions and choosing to be patient with my healing process. (Give your personal example.)

III. Relax/Meditate - Silent Moments of Connection:

Turn off the TV, cell phone, etc.

Write a gratitude statement. For example, it can simply be the ability to see the beauty of the earth. Write down a gratitude statement whenever you feel depressed.

IV. Be Grateful - Gratitude Journal Entry: Fill in the blank. "Today, I am thankful for ___________________."

Positivity Boulevard

9
Mid-day's Acceptance

Love is Patient

Today's working definition: **Patience**: calmness under pressure; persevering through trials with calm delight and mental relaxation, trusting God's word.

This peace-provoking act requires us to bear life's trails with calmness and peace. It requires us to accept the cyclical nature of life. In this section, you will learn to develop leadership skills that are critical to maintaining through your purposeful journey. This action also requires us to persevere with calmness and to expect a positive outcome (faith).

So, my journey to acceptance begins…

Acceptance is a peaceful act. When survivors learn to accept the loss of their loved one, we are well on the road to peaceful healing for wholeness. Life is cyclical, and every life form comes into and out of existence. In other words, life consists of an up and down cycle. For example, the sun rises and sets, the waves go up and down, and the leaves grow and then die in the fall. We have to accept this up and down cycle as a common denominator of the universe. Once we accept this as simply a fact of life, peace will reign. The Bible states, "There is a season for every activity under the sun, a time to be born and a time to die (Ecclesiastes 3:1-2).

Acceptance can be intellectual or emotional. In intellectual acceptance, the survivor understands the loss and sees the world as continuing to make sense. Emotional acceptance allows the survivor to find more pleasure than pain in remembering their loved one. In my experience, I obtained intellectual acceptance prior to emotional acceptance. Because my mom's death was very traumatic due to her short illness, her young age, our close relationship and my lack of mental preparation in the area of death, I had to work through a barrage of overwhelming emotions and feelings to reach emotional acceptance. Consequently, not until I was able to accept my loss was I able to begin to focus on the positive. I believe this acceptance propelled me to focus on the positives in my life. Ultimately, we must accept the fact that there are some things we cannot change. We can only change the way we react, so accept the facts of life although they may not seem fair.

~Fruits of Peace~

The Keys of Transforming Power

1. Spend quiet time and meditate on your desires

2. Give, Give, Give

3. Manage emotions - Emotional Intelligence (EI)

4. Practice acceptance - peaceful gift

5. Seek to help empower/improve their lives

6. Remain detached from the outcome

7. Wait patiently

Remember, God is fair, and acceptance leads to inner peace and wholeness (healing).

Reflection Exercise

Acceptance

The Power of Words:

I. Speak Positives - My Affirmation Statement:

Say it aloud and write the affirmation statement 7 times.

"I am accepting my loss so I can focus on the positive."

II. Serve Self and Others - My Love Walk:

Love always creates inner peace!

Today, I walked in love by accepting my loss and planning a special day for a loved one. (Give your personal example.)

III. Relax/Meditate - Silent Moments of Connection:

Write down where you want to be in 5, 10 and 15 years from now, both personally and professionally.

IV. Be Grateful - Gratitude Journal Entry: Fill in the blank. "Today, I am thankful for ___________________."

10
Mid-day's Self-Control

"But the fruits of the spirit are love, joy, peace and self-control."
(Galatians 5:22)

Self-control is essential to peaceful healing. Primarily, survivors must learn to control their negative emotions that accompany loss and adversity. Self-control is only possible if we take a moment to detach from our emotions and feelings and consciously choose non-negative responses. In essence, we must choose to be proactive, not reactive. This will require mental strength, which is developed by resisting our natural reaction. We have to choose to let peace be our decision maker and lead our responses. In the time of grieving, we should choose to exist in a state of harmony instead of a state of depression. This stress management strategy requires having a positive mindset.

So, my journey to self-control begins…

To respond in a peaceful way requires effective interpersonal communication, or some buffers to keep us from reacting in a negative way to others. Buffers assist us in detaching from not being led by negative emotions. The buffers can be prayer, affirmation, or reflective questioning. First, a survivor's prayer may be, "Guard my tongue, Lord." "Lord, help me to have a reaction that serves as an example of peace." Second, we can repeat affirmations until a feeling of peace and calmness returns. Affirmations are positive statements that can be said aloud or silently. They demonstrate the power of our words. The power of words was initially demonstrated in the beginning of the Bible. The Lord said, "Let there be light, sky, man" (Genesis 1-2). Everything on Earth was created by God's spoken word. I often use Bible verses as an affirmation statement. Affirmations increase mental fitness. Remember, the mind is a muscle, and mental exercise (affirmations) and resistance training builds mental strength. Lastly, when we feel out of control, we must conduct a mental interview and ask ourselves, "What is really going on here?" Oftentimes, what appears to be a problem on the surface is really due to underlying insecurities or fear. Consequently, maintaining self-control while being emotionally overwhelmed due to grieving is not always easy but, oftentimes, it can be done if we have buffers in place so we can choose to respond proactively in a positive manner. Remember, the Bible instructs us to be self-controlled and not easily angered.

We can overcome tests although we may not respond in peace every time to an adversity or loss, so accept this as a human fact and be patient with yourself. However, our aim should be balance, and if we are responding in love and peace more often than we can count it all joy.

Remember, we should walk in love with ourselves as well as others. It is easier to practice self-control if there is an abundance of self-love. This walk requires us to forgive ourselves, and thus free ourselves from additional emotional anxiety. As survivors, we should keep in mind the words of Abraham Lincoln, "Life is 10% of what happens to us and 90% how we respond."

In the next chapter, we will explore the different ways to heal such as self-love healing, holistic healing, confidence healing and empowered healing. These types of healing provide guidance for alternative, healthy ways of escape and comfort when grieving a loss of any kind.

Reflection Exercise

Self-Control

The Power of Words:

I. Speak Positives - My Affirmation Statement:

Say it aloud and write the affirmation statement 7 times.

"I am an example of peace and self-control."

II. Serve Self and Others - My Love Walk:

Love always creates inner peace!

Today, I demonstrated love by responding with a kind word to an adversary who was rude and disrespectful. (Give your personal example.)

III. Relax/Meditate-Silent Moments of Connection:

Turn off the TV, cell phone, etc.

Plan a "love celebration" for yourself. Remember, it is easier to practice self-control if there is an abundance of self-love.

IV. Be Grateful - Gratitude Journal Entry: Fill in the blank. "Today, I am thankful for ___________________."

Sunshine Parkway

11
Sunrise's Self-Healing

Love Does Not Envy

Today's working definition: **Non-Envy**: not wanting what others have.

This inner-peace-provoking act requires us to not feel resentment due to our desires for the fruits—possessions or qualities—of another. It also requires us to be grateful for what we have and know that we have the power to receive even greater gifts.

So, my journey to non-envy/judgement begins…

The most critical component of self-healing is self-love. Self-love involves directing loving acts toward self. This stress management tactic helps us to remain calm and make rational decisions in all situations. During the grieving process and beyond, survivors need to focus on self-love to heal. We need to cultivate a positive attitude of self-love and implement self-pampering practices.

Cultivating a positive attitude of self-love includes a demonstration of loving acts, i.e. patience, kindness, self-control, non-envy and forgiveness. First, we must learn to be patient with ourselves during the grieving process. Healing takes time. Oftentimes, when we lose a loved one, job or income, etc. a part of us feels lost or incomplete. Therefore, practicing patience is critical. Remember, we are simply works in progress.

Second, self-healing or self-love requires us to be kind to ourselves. Practice making positive statements about yourself daily. Your daily affirmations can serve as a tool to build self after the death of a loved one. Oftentimes, I used biblical affirmations, for example, "I am more than a conqueror" (Romans 8:37).

Third, survivors can heal themselves by being self-controlled. Self-control is simply self-discipline. It is obtained by implementing mental fitness skills. These skills are built by resisting our natural tendency to react to a negative stimulus in a negative way. If we lose control and react negatively, we will have additional negative emotions or feelings to cope with mentally, such as sadness and regret. Very often, we have not responded appropriately. When we practice self-control, we experience inner peace. So, save yourself for additional mental anguish and practice self-control. It can be very rewarding and therapeutic.

Fourth, survivors should not envy others who appear to have loved ones or other things present. Oftentimes, the relationships are not what they appear on the surface. In other words, the grass appears to be greener on the other side of the fence. Remember, it is only the position of the light at that moment. Other families or relationships may seem physically intact, with loved ones physically present, but mentally, emotionally, spiritually and socially, they are absent. All they have is the physical presence of a person or an empty shell. Therefore, do not envy others. Consider yourself fortunate if you did lose someone with whom you shared a complete "holistic" relationship. Often, we question ourselves, "Why did this happen to me?" The answer to this question is that God, in his infinite wisdom, decided it was time to call "his" loved one home. I'd like to think he had some angel duty for them. Don't envy others, simply seek acceptance and your healing will begin.

Lastly, forgiveness is paramount to self-healing. We have to forgive ourselves as well as others. Oftentimes, we blame ourselves, or we blame the doctors, gun control legislation, family or friends. We feel that *if only I was able to save my loved one, he or she would still be with us.* Remember, the savior role was reserved for Jesus Christ, not us. To heal and gain peace, we must accept that there is a time for everything, and death is inevitable for us all. So, stop playing the blame game because it hinders your healing. Forgive and free yourself to heal.

Although we have hectic schedules in the 21st century and time is a valuable resource, we must be aware that taking the time to pamper ourselves will lead to inner peace and wholeness. Planning is a peaceful skill that is critical in time management, so plan time to love yourself. Self-renewal or pampering is essential to self-healing. It helps survivors rejuvenate themselves after the death of a loved one. This renewal or rejuvenation requires the use of pampering techniques. To discover how to pamper yourself, answer the question, what activity makes me feel really good, joyful and peaceful? The key word is "me." It should be solely for self. It's OK to seek to put ourselves first, as long as we are not seeking to serve self only.

First, we will address what I refer to as "mental pampering," or activities that cater to our inner spirit. For example, I enjoy reading, jogging in the park, listening to inspirational music, relaxing on the sofa with a candle lit watching my favorite shows or movies and overlooking the oceanfront with a late evening jog. I believe nature has healing properties, thus observing nature gives me a feeling of inner peace and wholeness. That's why I prefer jogging at a park with natural scenery rather than at a school track. Recently, my mental pampering has consisted of daily morning walks through my neighborhood. It has been extremely mentally calming and therapeutic during the quarantine due to the viral pandemic. When was the last time you picked up a buttercup or blew a dandelion? Remember, a natural setting soothes the spirit. So, experience the inner healing only nature can provide.

Next, survivors need to take time to pamper their outer body. I refer to this as "physical pampering." I always feel good when I get my head pampered. It can be a home job or a trip to the beauty salon; it does not matter. It appears that once I pamper myself, my self-esteem or self-confidence goes up a notch. My second favorite is my nails. When my nails are well-manicured, I feel good also. Recently, I committed myself to develop a pampering plan. I have started to make my routine bathing a special pampering ritual for myself. I make it special by using candles, incense and body oils. I use chamomile, jasmine and lavender body oils in my bath water or body gel when showering because they have relaxing, peace-provoking properties. I also use eucalyptus because it is primarily known for its healing properties. These oils are derived from natural plant sources. I use a planner to make sure I allocate time for pampering. I believe planners are peace-provoking tools because they help manage time more efficiently so our day can run more smoothly; they also give our life order. I have found that taking the time to mentally and physically pamper myself increases my feeling of calmness and inner peace. Also, all negative emotions that accompany grieving seem to fade away. Thus, survivors need to be conscious about integrating self-healing or renewal practices frequently in their schedules.

I met Regal in one of my "I Love Me" seminars. She had a peaceful presence. She shared that she had recently been released from prison; however, while in bondage, she discovered her gift of singing. I shared with her that, often, when we are in bondage, oppressed, or in a position of stillness, our spirit has an opportunity to receive guidance and tap into our inner wisdom due to the minimization of physical or worldly distractions. She is now working, taking classes and sharing her gift to bring joy to others. I encouraged Regal to practice self-love activities through her process of restoration.

Consequently, positive attitudes of self-love along with self-pampering practices will lead survivors well on the road to inner healing or wholeness. Learn to love, comfort and be your own best friend.

~Fruits of Peace~

Self-Love

Pampering is…

A holistic practice that nurtures the body, mind and spirit.

An experience that brings joy, calm delight and inner peace

A healing ritual that moves one from fear and worry to peace and faith

1. **Develop a "Self-love first" consciousness**
2. **Create a pampering toolbox**
3. **Plan pampering time**
4. **Practice positive self-talk**
5. **Take action**
6. **Enjoy!**

Remember, self-healing is the result of self-love and self-pampering. There is only one you.

Reflection Exercise

Self-Healing

The Power of Words

I. Speak Positives - My Affirmation Statement:

Say aloud and write the affirmation statement 7 times.

"I am continually filling my cup and it is running over with love"

II. Serve Self and Others - My Love walk:

Love always creates inner peace and healing!

Today, I demonstrated self-love by spending an afternoon in the park reading, jogging, watching the ducks in the lake, relaxing on the sofa with a lit candle while watching my favorite show/movie.

My personal example: _______________________

III. Relax/Meditate - Silent Moments of Connection:

Turn off the TV, cell phone, etc.

Take an "I am special" bath with scented bubble bath, oils, candles, incense and soft music. Enjoy!

IV. Be Grateful - Gratitude Journal Entry: Fill in the blank.
"Today, I am thankful for _______________."

12
Sunrise's Holistic Healing

"*May your whole spirit, soul and body be kept.*"
(Thessalonians 5:23)

Healing results in wholeness, and it is God's desire for us to be whole in mind, body and spirit. When we experience loss of any kind, we feel a part of us is missing or that we are not whole. To recapture the feeling of wholeness, we need to take part in holistic activities that focus on different areas—mental, emotional, physical, social and spiritual—and it will result in self-empowered healing. In essence, this stress management strategy helps to restore balance or wholeness into our lives so we can endure our purposeful leadership assignment.

Nationally, with the increase of gun violence, many people have to deal with the traumatic experience of losing a loved one or classmate at a young age. Across the country, within the last five years, there have been approximately fifteen different cases of school shootings. This trend can be extremely emotionally overwhelming for a young person because they have not developed mental skills to cope with this kind of adversity. In addition, they do not expect their peers to die so young. Unfortunately, I believe expectancy may be changing. Working as a teacher in high schools, I have had the experience of hearing high school students discuss many of their friends who have been shot and/or killed. Unfortunately, it appears to be becoming a common occurrence. With this sad trend, there is a strong need for grief counseling to help today's youth understand their feelings so that negative backlash or behavior does not occur. Also, it appears with the increase in school gun violence, their respect for the value of human life is decreasing. It is dangerous to think about the repercussions that can occur from a generation that does not value human life. Also, parents increasingly have to deal with the pain of losing a child due to gun violence. Their grief is intense because, not only did they lose a child, but they also lost the hope of what their child could have become. The pain that the youth and adult survivor experience is often overwhelming. Also, workplace gun violence and incurable diseases such as AIDS, cancer, viruses, etc. are taking lives daily. The need for holistic healing is becoming increasingly important.

First, mental or emotional holistic healing involves programming our minds to focus on positive memories as well as choosing the correct response when grieving. Because grieving is a mental struggle, mental fitness holistic activities are important. Resisting our natural tendency to react negatively in the grieving process—denial, anger, blame, depression—can be critical. Mentally fit people are aware that these emotions are natural when dealing with grief, but they choose not to be led by these emotions. They use mental buffers such as affirmation statements to cushion their response. The survivors realize that, during this mental struggle, they may not be emotionally stable. Therefore, they make a conscious effort to be mindful of making negative choices that could lead to excessive negative behaviors such as excessive worrying, substance abuse or promiscuity to numb the pain of their loss. They are aware that they may be especially vulnerable and sensitive during this time. Also, during this time, they should not make any major decision like leaving a job, relocating, getting married or divorced because the pain and the overwhelming emotions can interfere with logical decision-making. Primarily, we need to program our minds to detach from our feelings. We should determine if our actions are based on feelings or if we need to detach from our feelings so they will not lead us astray.

During my mom's illness, I was working at a healthcare company. In my cubicle, I had a post-it with a quote from Abraham Lincoln, and I looked at it daily. The quote was, "Life is 10% what happens to us and 90% how we respond." This quote became a daily affirmation statement for me that I would say silently to myself throughout my mom's illness. It gave me the mental strength and inner peace I needed to persevere despite my pain. I believe this mental exercise led to my healing or feeling of wholeness. Remember, your mind is your most powerful resource!

Second, physical holistic healing involves proper nutrition and exercise. During the grieving process especially, survivors should make sure they are eating nutritious, high alkaline foods (primarily fruits and vegetables) and exercising. Due to the mental and emotional turmoil experienced during this time, stress can be overwhelming. Unfortunately, during the grieving period, many survivors lose their desire to eat, sleep or take part in any social activities. We have to resist this tendency and focus on the benefits of physical fitness. When we have a healthy diet of well-balanced means, our brain, as well as our overall body, get the nutrients needed to function properly. In addition, proper exercise serves as a release for negative emotions and endorphins, a chemical hormone in the brain. When endorphins are released, they give us a good feeling or emotional high known as the "runners high."

After I lost my mom and during her suffering, I religiously went to the park and ran miles as a form of stress release. Often, during my run, tears would flow down my cheeks as I reworked the memories of my mom and our trips talking and laughing through the same park. I wore sunglasses and I told myself that no one knew I was crying—they would probably think it was just sweat flowing down my face. However, during her short illness of three months I was not eating much, primarily because I was so busy trying to manage everything. I did not have time to eat. In other words, eating was not a high priority.

However, when I did eat, I ate plenty of healthy foods; the salad bar was my favorite. Because it was summer, fruits and vegetables were ripe and delicious. Fortunately, after my mom passed, I began to regain the weight I had lost. Oftentimes, because of the mental struggle inevitable in grief and an improper diet and/or lack of exercise, many survivors experience physical ailments such as headaches, ulcers, etc. I did not, and I believe this was due to the physical holistic healing habits I implemented as I transitioned through my grieving period.

Third, social holistic healing, which involves connecting or spending time cultivating relationships with others, is extremely important in the grieving process. Oftentimes, survivors seek to be isolated from others when they are grieving. This isolation is not healthy because it often results in the survivor being alone, dwelling on the memories of their late loved one. It is during this time that social holistic activities are critical. We need to be out socializing and engaging in relationships because they can serve as a positive diversion from our loss. Therefore, survivors are encouraged to seek out social activities such as going to dinner, movies, shopping, etc. during this grieving period, not being left alone. Also, by engaging in a social life, we get opportunities to express feelings and emotions. Having someone to listen can be very therapeutic in the grieving process. Most importantly, we need to be comforted during this time by family and friends.

During my mom's illness, I went to dinner, movies and visited my friend's family. I believe it was the positive diversion I needed because it took my mind off the reworkings of the most recent memories of my mom, which was her suffering. After she passed, my friend and I got engaged, so, with planning the wedding, graduate school and work, as well as our dates, I was so busy, and my mind was free from negative thoughts that accompany grief. I believe these interactions kept me transitioning through the grieving process with peace. I still had my moments when I would cry due to the pain of losing my mom. I had never cried in front of the man I was dating, so this was very different, but trying to maintain the hard exterior was too difficult during my grieving period. I tried to suppress my emotions like I had often done during her illness, but when my mom died, I could not suppress my feelings as much. However, I believe my social connections with friends and family made this traumatic experience more bearable.

Fourth, spiritual holistic healing involves connecting to our higher power—God. I believe this is the most important component to peaceful healing. We should seek to have balance in all areas—mental, emotional, physical, social and spiritual. However, if there is imbalance, it should be in the favor of holistic practices, because losing a loved one affects our inner spirit. We should seek to lift our spirits with spiritual activities that lead to holistic healing. During this time, survivors should increase prayer time (talking to God) and meditation activities (listening to God), as well as incorporate moments of silence.

At first, during my mom's brief illness, which led to her death, I would often pray, "God, give me strength to endure and to be strong for my mom." My prayers were answered throughout her illness, even though making the funeral arrangements. However, the weeks after the funeral was when my grieving was more intense. My prayer became, "God, help me to carry on," because I felt like someone had taken out part of my heart; in other words, I did not feel whole. That prayer was answered as well. Although I went through all the stages of grieving, by the grace and mercy of God, I was still able to keep my emotions in balance, for the most part, to function on the job and complete graduate school. Overall, the spiritual activities I practiced were a lot of prayer, church fellowship, mediation and moments of quiet time. My prayer life expanded to include prayers of praise, thanking God for what he has done; petitioning, asking God to give me strength and endurance; and protest, asking God to fulfill the promise of his word in my life. Throughout my grieving, I attended our church for the spiritual nourishment I needed to persevere. Next, I would take notes at church on the sermon topic and re-read the Bible verse to think or meditate on how it was relevant to my life experience. Lastly, my bible reading was always done in silence. I could not have any external noise or distractions, for example, no TV, no music, no cell phone. I would turn my phone's ringer off. Consequently, in the reflection exercises at the end of each chapter in this guide include moments of silence. I believe silence is critical to living a peaceful existence and to inner healing. Also, I am an advocate of the end-of-the-workday siesta, or little nap. I believe this quiet time gives me the opportunity to recharge and renew myself. In essence, it is necessary for survivors to incorporate all four practices—prayer, fellowship, mediation and moments of silence, during the grieving period to heal. Remember, emotional stability is our spiritual inheritance.

An excellent Bible model of holistic healing is King David when he was grieving for his son's illness and later death. During his son's illness, David mourned his son. He prayed alone and fasted or refused to eat. Isolation and inability to act are typical behaviors when grieving for a loved one. However, when his son died, he sought a holistic approach to healing. He got up, chose to change his focus (mental healing), worshiped the Lord (spiritual healing), ate (physical healing) and comforted his wife (social healing).

~Fruits of Peace~

Holistic Healing

Health is the state of wholeness achieved by balance

Holistic Activities:

★ **Mental/Emotional - programming positive thoughts**

★ **Physical - proper diet and exercise**

★ **Social - confidence and relationship building**

★ **Spiritual - community service**

Our life's peaceful purpose requires us to live in balance.

Dis-ease is a holistic imbalance.

Healing is the act of restoring balance and begins in the mind with positive, healthy thoughts and confident expectations.

LOVE HEALS!!!

Remember, we cannot change the past. Our responsibility is to look to the light of the future and enjoy the present gift. Practicing the holistic healing activities mentioned in this section helps us to heal successfully with inner peace. Soon, you will be singing the lyrics from Beyoncé and Destiny's Child's popular song, "I'm a Survivor".

Reflection Exercise

Holistic Healing

The Power of Words:

I. Speak Positives - My Affirmation Statement:

Say aloud and write the affirmation statement 7 times.

"I am practicing a holistic activity right now."

II. Serve Self and Others - My Love Walk:

Love always creates inner peace and healing!

Today, I demonstrated love by spending time participating in holistic activities, for example:

➤ Mentally (emotionally): I chose the appropriate responses to grieving emotions.

➤ Physically: I went for a walk through the neighborhood.

➤ Socially: I went to the movies with a friend.

➤ Spiritually: I listened to inspirational music.

My personal example: ___________________."

III. Relax/Meditate - Silent Moments of Connections:

Turn off the TV, cell phone, etc.

Go to the park, walk or jog, and take time to appreciate the beautiful surroundings.

IV. Be Grateful - Gratitude Journal Entry: Fill in the blank. "Today, I am thankful for ___________________."

13
Sunrise's Self-Confidence Healing

"I can do all things through Christ who strengthens me."
(Philippians 4.13)

After we have experienced a loss, we have to focus on rebuilding our self-confidence, or positive inner knowing. This is critical because, often, when we experience loss, we feel hopeless and worthless because we could not control the outcome. Also, when we experience a loss, we feel a part of us is empty. Remember, self-confidence, or having a positive self-esteem, is a mental quality that can be learned and is critical for purpose-based leadership. In the grieving process, the negative feelings or emotions can lead to depression, or a low, sad state of mind. Confident survivors avoid feelings of depression by focusing on positive solutions to cope with loss and to propel them through the grieving process. Self-confidence involves having a strong belief in our personal power. This belief leads to peaceful healing. We should see ourselves as leaders and seek enjoyment, mental peace or calmness, positive mental programming tactics and social interactions.

First, self-confident survivors see themselves as leaders with an essential vision/mission. Our self-healing goal is driven by our value to persevere despite loss. We believe we must take responsibility for our own healing and utilize our strengths, talents and skills to do so.

Second, self-confident survivors spend the majority of their time doing something they enjoy. This act increases self-confidence. We should know that everything we do in life could either increase or decrease one's self confidence. So, we should be conscious to choose activities that we enjoy, increasing our evaluation of ourselves. We should be committed to living a life to its fullest and being the best, we can be.

Third, self-confident survivors seek mental peace and calmness. We are aware that this act also increases our self-confidence. Mental fitness is key; therefore, our aim is to keep all negative thoughts or influences out and to focus on keeping a clear, calm and peaceful mind.

Fourth, self-confident survivors seek positive mental programming tactics to increase self-confidence. These tactics include affirmation statements and visualization exercises, such as surrounding themselves with positive people. As I mentioned earlier, affirmations, positive self-talk, or inner dialogue, are essential for building mental strength in adverse situations. In positive visualization, we mentally picture ourselves as whole or free from negative emotions that accompany the grieving process. Also, we seek to surround ourselves with positive people, books, etc. These mental programming tactics rebuild one's self esteem reduced by losses.

Lastly, self-confident survivors have the desire and ability to get along with all kinds of people. Embracing diversity leads to improvement in your life as well as the lives of others. They are aware that socially disconnected people are weaker holistically.

~Fruits of Peace~

Confidence is...

Maintaining confidence in the midst of loss or adversity to achieve a desired purpose or goal while trusting in inner infinite wisdom.

Inner knowing without any doubt!

Thinking Confidently....

- ❖ Strong belief in personal power
- ❖ Firm assurance of mind
- ❖ Inner trusting
- ❖ Positive self-knowing

Speaking Confidently...

- ❖ Speak with authority and conviction
- ❖ Varied tone high/low
- ❖ Have clear pronunciation

Projecting Confidence...

- ❖ Smile gently
- ❖ Align posture
- ❖ Make eye contact

Remember, everyone experiences temporary defeats or losses, and most of us become emotionally overwhelmed when dealing with adversity. We need to focus on our strengths and spend time doing what self-confident survivors do to rebuild or increase our self-confidence. Keep in mind, it is our reaction that holds the key to self-confident healing.

Reflection Exercise

Self-Confidence Healing

The Power of Words

I. Speak Positives - My Affirmation Statement:

Say aloud and write 7 times.

"I am doing what I enjoy, therefore, I have an abundance of confidence."

II. Serve Self and Others - My Love Walk:

I will demonstrate love by attentively listening to a friend without interruption.

My personal example: ______________________

III. Relax/Meditate - Silent Moments of Connection:

Turn off the TV, cell phone, etc.

Spend time participating in your hobby. For example, tennis, jogging, crocheting or going to the mall. To create a hobby, simply routinely seek to do an activity that you enjoy.

IV. Be Grateful - Gratitude Journal Entry: Fill in the blank.
"Today, I am thankful for ______________________."

14
Sunrise's Empowered Healing

"For God did not give us the spirit of fear, but a spirit of love, power and a sound mind..."
(2 Timothy 1:7)

Being empowered provides peaceful healing. Empowerment is the act of displaying personal power. Purpose-based leaders must believe that they have been endowed with power to fulfill their earthly assignment (life's purpose). Spending time participating in holistic healing activity increases this personal power. As we implement acts that improve mental, emotional, physical, social and spiritual development, our personal power will increase significantly. A survivor's aim should be to acquire balance in these areas. However, if there is an imbalance in the time spent in these areas, it should lean to the area of the spiritual practices. Because, when we experience loss, it primarily affects our spirits. So, to heal spiritually is of utmost importance. A biblical example of empowerment can be found in the book of Acts, which focuses on Jesus' disciples' demonstration of miraculous works. After spending time with Jesus, they were empowered to heal. They began to exhibit an increase in personal power. This reveals the healing power that comes primarily from connecting to the Higher Power. Therefore, as we connect to our higher power source, our personal power will grow. As I practiced holistic healing activities, especially in the spiritual arena, my power to persevere in the spiritual area, my power to persevere despite the loss increased and, later, I was empowered to help encourage others to realize the power within them to heal during the grieving process.

~Fruits of Peace~

Empowerment

★ It is the ability to make decisions independently

★ It focuses on one's choice

★ It is the act of displaying personal power

★ It is activated when we respond with love, peace and kindness

★ It increases when we connect with the infinite wisdom within.

**Use your POWER to improve your life and the lives of others.
Be Empowered!!!**

In my "Empowerment Self-Confidence" workshop, one of the participants excused herself when she became overwhelmed with emotions. Later, she shared with me she had recently lost her father. Losing a loved one is an emotionally and spiritually draining experience. I had shared my personal testimony about enduring the loss of my mom to cancer. I shared that it was the most traumatic crisis I had experienced. I also shared with them the path I chose to heal and empower myself. Ultimately, my healing resulted from focusing on spirit. As a result, I became empowered and confident by choosing to release the pain of the past. I encouraged her as well as the other workshop participants to do the same so they can heal and be victorious too.

Remember, empowerment requires us to put our positive personal power to work for ourselves as well as others. We are all powerful beings; however, we often don't realize the power within ourselves. Stay connected to your power source and get busy creating positive change.

Reflection Exercise

Empowerment

The Power of Words

I. Speak Positives - My Affirmation Statement:

Say aloud and write the affirmation statement 7 times.

"I am empowering others to live a peaceful life."

II. Serve Self and Others - My Love Walk:

Love always creates inner peace and healing!

Today, I demonstrated love by encouraging others to recognize the power within.

My personal example: _____________________.

III. Relax and Meditate - Silent Moments of Connection:

Take a "power nap" in the afternoon or evening and feel your power increase.

IV. Be Grateful-Gratitude Journal Entry: Fill in the blank. "Today, I am thankful for _____________________."

15
Sunrise's Gracious Legacy

"Give thanks in all circumstances"
(1 Thessalonians 5:18)

Survivors need to look at the gifts they received from their losses, loved one, job, income, etc. We need to cultivate an attitude of gratitude by simply being grateful for the gifts/love we have received. Reflect on the many ways your life has been enriched. Upon reflecting on the loss of a loved one, for example, ask yourself, "What do I remember most about my loved one?" The answer to this question will reveal his or her legacy.

What I remember most about my mom was her love, unselfish giving and encouragement. This is the wonderful legacy she left for me. I believe one's legacy is a divine gift. I am very grateful for our time together, especially for her example of love. Now, it is my turn to pass these gifts on to my children.

Be grateful for your loved one's presence, income, God's provision, the miraculous innate healing power of the human body, etc. in the past, present and future. Remember, one's spirit never dies and our gift to God is what we do with our life!

Although most of the examples provided in the *Adversity Turnpike - Grieving the Sunset* section pertained to healing from the most difficult losses we experience on our early journey, the loss of a loved one, the grieving process is the same for all losses we experience. The losses may be financial due to loss of a job, position, personal health issue, etc. However, the way through and out is also the same! Survivors confidently and peacefully walk through life adversities grieving processes by practicing the holistic—mental, emotional, physical, social and spiritual—practices or stress management strategies detailed in this section, and you will persevere and be victorious! Remember, in all these things, you are more than conquerors through him who loved us (Roman 8.37).

Reflection Exercise

A Gracious Legacy

The Power of Words

I. Speak Positively - My Affirmation Statement:

Say aloud and write the affirmation statement 7 times.

"I am very grateful for the love I have received."

II. Serve Self and Others - My Love Walk:

I demonstrated love by writing a love note to a loved one, simply expressing why I am grateful for their presence in my life.

My personal example: ___________________

III. Relax/Meditate - Silent Moments of Connection:

Turn off the TV, cell phone etc.

Take 30 minutes of quality time and listen to relaxing music.

IV. Be Grateful-Gratitude Journal Entry: Fill in the blank. "Today, I am thankful for ___________."

Relationships Highway

~Peaceful Legacy of Light~

*This section provides relationship skills for harmonious interactions. It details the loving acts that motivated me to fulfill my peaceful purpose (empowerment). Developing and maintaining rich relationships is critical to the fulfillment of one's purpose. In this section, I will illustrate two critical, purposeful relationships—one's significant other and children. Focusing on **Humility**, **Forgiveness** and **Kindness** propelled me into my destiny. In essence, being an example of love, peace and balance while sharing information that will improve the lives of others will be my legacy, my light in the world.*

16
The Love Relationship Harvest

Love is Humble

Today's working definition: **Meekness** means practicing humility.

This peace-provoking act requires one to think of serving others with the abilities and talents you received; it is the essence of humility. This often results in pure joy. However, we must remember, it is very important to honor or love self so we can serve others with love. We cannot serve what we do not have.

A person who is pursuing his/her purpose knows the greatest of all is the servant of all. Therefore, they seek to serve others with their gifts, skills and abilities.

So, my journey to becoming selfless, or humble, begins with my third most important relationship, following my Heavenly Father—my earthly parents.

My love story begins with Mr. Tall, Dark and Handsome, the exterior packaging I'd always liked. We met when one of my high school friends encouraged me to go to 'Ladies Night Out' after I had shared some details of my mom's illness. I very rarely revealed my feelings and all the transitions in my childhood. In the past, just when I would develop close relationships, oftentimes, I would have to move again. I believed this contributed to my lack of trust in social relationships. Also, I rarely revealed my feelings because I believed it was a sign of immaturity. I thought that strong, mature people were able to conceal their emotions, especially feelings of weakness. I was very cautious in my relationships, as the Bible encourages us. Be prudent in all relationships (Proverbs 12:26). Somewhat reluctantly, my girlfriend and I got dolled up and went to "Ladies Night Out." My mom also encouraged me to go, saying, "I will be OK. Stop worrying about me." My friend introduced me to her friend, and he, in turn, introduced me to his coworker/friend, Mr. Tall Dark and Handsome, a.k.a. whom I believe was my soul mate. This was the beginning of the tumultuous journey. He asked for my phone number, but it was my rule not to give men my phone number because I lived alone. So, I took his number instead. However, the next morning, I threw his phone number away because I thought my life was already complicated enough with caring for a terminally ill parent, working a full-time job and attending graduate school. The next day, my girlfriend called and stated he wanted me to call him. I cooked dinner for my mom, and we talked, as usual, about my ladies' night adventure. I got his phone number again and called. I thought maybe I needed a positive diversion. We began to date. His friendship was welcomed as my mom's condition worsens. After work, school and daily visits to the hospital, we would have dinner. I thought he was a good listener, which was what I needed at the time. However, in the past, I preferred men with stimulating conversation about racial issues, world events, politics, religion, etc. Three months after our relationship began, my mom passed—within 60 days, just as the oncologist had predicted. My friend had just bought a house the month before we met and had asked me to move in with him. I shared this with my mom, and she said, "Do whatever makes you happy."

Neither my soul mate nor I have ever had a serious, long-term close relationship or marriage, so our experiences were new. Together, we went through the school of hard knocks. Initially we did not share our thoughts because we did not know how to or if we should; this was such a new journey for us. Shortly after we were married, oftentimes, we went for weeks without communicating. Later, we were told how important communication is to a relationship, so I began to talk, talk, talk, to no avail. The more I shared my thoughts and fears, the more distant he became. I viewed this as a sign of rejection. Later, I was led to read about the different communication styles of women and men. I had read that men have a tendency to go into the cave or deal with problems by being left alone. Women, on the other hand, have a tendency to be very expressive when confronting problems. It was comforting to know that what we were experiencing was typical, although I did not like it. I learned to accept the differences as a part of the dynamics of a healthy relationship. We should welcome the differences in our soulmate because it brings balance and completeness to our lives. Therefore, we should invite a relationship based on truth.

Shortly after I completed graduate school, he asked me if I wanted to start a family. In the past, I had been joking with him about having a little "J." I was elated when our son was born. He was a perfect blend of both of us. Although the growth issues and power struggle continued to surface, the new little one served as a diversion until the pressure of balancing new responsibilities--work, home, childcare— surfaced. Again, I searched for answers to help through prayer, church activities and by reading relationship books, which led me to understand what we were experiencing was normal. However, the cycle continued. I realized that rejection caused damaged emotions. As the cycle continued, I knew I had to serve as a catalyst for change. I believe, because women are nurturers, we often have to nurture our relationships. I attempted to implement some of the information I had read about making the other person feel special. Consequently, I learned that having peace was more important than being right! I also learned that it is not our job to fix anyone. Our task is simply to provide them with a peaceful example of love, encouragement and guidance on how to transform themselves with the power within. Thus, I changed my mental focus and tried to be an example of peace, which I learned we cannot do alone without the Prince of Peace, Jesus Christ. I began to focus on my life's purpose, sharing my gift of encouraging and empowering others to fulfill their peaceful destiny by sharing information that improves lives.

So many of us desire close, fulfilling relationships, but are we truly ready? Being committed, unconditionally, (no matter what) is what marriage is all about. Also, I learned that having our priorities in the right order is critical to a peaceful, loving relationship. The order should be: God, spouse, children, family and friends. The Bible states, a man shall leave his father and mother and be united to his wife, and the two will become one flesh (Matthew 19:5, 6). Who do you talk to first concerning your marriage or mate? Is it God, your family, your friends, or your spouse? Thus, walking in love, kindness, self-control and patience will create a peaceful, loving relationship. Consequently, I believe we need to view this as the most important decision we make, in addition to deciding how we can make a difference in service to the world through faith and empowerment. Oftentimes, we think we are ready. We look at the outward packaging and hastily make a decision, but I believe it requires much prayer and careful thought because anything worthwhile is never without trails, but with God as our anchor, nothing is unbearable.

~Fruits of Peace~

A Heavenly Marriage on Earth

1. Pray continuously for desired characteristics you want in a mate

2. Communicate love and appreciation

3. Give thanks for qualities you presently enjoy

4. Forgive—Not everything is not fair, but God is!

Marriage does not guarantee happiness...

Happiness is found by dwelling on spiritual truths!

Remember, love is the greatest gift. Giving of yourself through love is a noble act. Seek to be humble in your relationship and you will receive inner peace. However, be mindful that the source you give may not always be the same source you receive from, but you will be rewarded abundantly. In other words, life doesn't always appear to be fair, but God is fair. When we reap what we sow while focusing on spirit, we will experience pure joy as well as inner peace and empowerment.

Reflection Exercise

Love is Selfless

The Power of Words:

I. Speak Positives - My Affirmation Statement

Say it aloud and write the affirmation statement 7 times.

"I am humble and, therefore, experiencing an abundance of joy with my soul mate."

II. Serve Self and Others - My Love Walk:

Love always creates inner peace!

Today, I walked in love by rejecting my desire to express my opinion on what I believe was right. Instead, I chose peace.

Give your personal example:

III. Relax/Meditate - Silent Moment of Connection:

Turn off the TV, cell phone, etc.

Spend a peaceful evening pampering yourself/soul mate. Be creative.

IV. Be Grateful-Gratitude Journal Entry: Fill in the blank. "Today, I am thankful for ___________________."

17
Peaceful Purpose Fulfilled Empowerment

Love Keeps No Wrongs…

Today's working definition: **Forgiveness** means not repaying evil with evil, but with a good deed, knowing you will be rewarded and free.

This purpose-based leadership skill is critical for successfully navigating through life's journey. Unforgiveness hurts you more than the person you are not forgiving. It binds us, poisons our thoughts and hinders us from progressing to the next level in our purpose. Let it go!

Finding and pursuing our purpose will result in total fulfillment of inner peace, confidence, joy and abundance. My trials, the rejection I experienced in marriage and work as I navigated to and through my journey prompted me to search for answers for survival as well as perseverance.

So, my journey with forgiveness begins…

Searching for answers and direction, I engaged, once again, in my favorite pastime—reading. I read everything I could get my hands on for guidance. I read spiritual literature, self-help books, and psychology-based books to fight these battles or rejection in my personal and professional life. I learned that there is a direct link between playing the blame game and rejection. Therefore, I could not blame the system's politics, my father, or my mate for the rejection I was experiencing because it was simply a part of life's learning school. Jesus himself experienced rejection. The purpose is to shape us into our purposeful destiny. It gives us an opportunity to grow. I believe I had to change my focus from the world's system and people to my inner ability to grow and rise above life's circumstances. I was again tapping into the power within (empowerment). I believe, if I wanted favor instead of rejection, I must remain blameless. Also, if I want favor, I must be an example of peace by demonstrating faith and appropriate behavior. In other words, if I did not do what God asked me first (obedience)—see my purpose/calling—he would not be obligated to answer the petitions of my heart. I believe that blaming is simply judging and, oftentimes, complaining. As I mentioned in the previous section of this book, *Grieving the Sunset*, blaming is a negative emotion that is an integral part of the grieving process. I found out that blaming took away my inner peace. I reflected on the basic biblical rules; judge not and complain not. Thus, I decided to guard my tongue and try to stay away from negative chatter such as gossiping, blaming and complaining as much as possible. Instead, I began to focus on positive speech, such as encouraging and complimenting. Also, I learned to replace blaming with praise, so, when I am in an adverse situation and have a natural tendency to blame others for the negative outcome or rejection, I simply thank God, knowing that the closed door is redirecting me to my abundant, peace-filled blessing.

The lessons I learned from rejection or the downward experiences are as follows: first, we must pray for those who reject us. They are viewed as our enemy but are simply growth opportunities or blessings in disguise. Remember that enemies are simply a part of life's school. They can be inside (our attitudes or responses) as well as outside (other people or things). Therefore, it is our responsibility to develop skills to respond to their attacks effectively so we can be victorious, keeping in mind that the battle belongs to the Lord. We can overcome adverse situations with love and kindness. Secondly, I look for the light, or the positive side, the lesson and count it all as joy. I did this by asking myself two questions: What is there to be learned? And how can I improve from this experience? I learned that it is OK and natural to sometimes feel hurt and get angry but respond prayerfully and proactively with kindness to separate your behavior from your emotions. If you cannot, flee. Lastly, rejection, or what we call a negative experience, teaches us to take responsibility or our lives and seek holistic, mind, body and spirit balance. Imbalance causes our focus to be unclear.

I have experienced rejection many times in lieu of professional promotion. I worked on the same job for ten years that I initially did not want because it was not in my chosen career path, but I took it to get my foot in the corporate door. After my first year, I attempted aggressively to move up the corporate ladder, but no promotion was gained. As a result, I went up north because I was told jobs were more plentiful. Later, I returned home and received countless rejection letters from my northern job hunt. I became discouraged. This encouraging and discouraging cycle continued for over a decade. So, I decided to pursue graduate school to make myself more marketable in corporate America. The rejection I experienced made me seek to look within. I continued graduate school and then sought employment in field education to no avail. I also experienced rejection in the education arena because I was not certified. That's when the vicious cycle began again, unrest job search, followed by rejection, stop job search.

After ten years of working in the same stagnant position and dealing with countless rejections, I decided, with much prayer, to take what I called a "faith walk." I decided to place my confidence in God and pursue my vision, a training and consulting business, One Focus Empowerment. I believe that, with confidence, having a firm belief in my God-given ability and talent, my true purpose was revealed. Now my task was to talk with confidence, and project it with my actions; thus, my "faith walk" became a reality in the spring of 1999.

Here is the process I went through to bring my vision into reality: rejection, spiritual strengthening, reflection and action. First, I experienced countless rejections, which helped me to continue to search and look deeper within for answers to my purpose. I am a believer that we all have the answers within us. However, we simply need to be still (at peace) and listen to our hearts and inner spirit. Second, I increasingly sought spiritual guidance. My Bible reading increased substantially as I searched for answers to my pattern of rejection. During this time, I received a clearer vision of how I was to serve the world. I believe this spiritual quest of stillness propelled me to seek deeper within myself. Third, I began to reflect more on my life's experiences for clues to my life's purpose. This reflection resulted in a self-imposed evaluation or assessment that consisted of a series of questions. For example, what do I enjoy most—hobbies? (Reading). What were my favorite subjects in school? (History and English). In what career path was I employed? (Marketing/Sales, Healthcare, Education). What qualities did my favorite teachers or corporate managers have? (Kindness, Fairness, Encouragement, Professionalism, and being well-informed or well-read in his or her field). These life evaluating questions and answers enabled me to listen to my life and identify what I enjoyed—my gift, passions and peaceful purpose. Ultimately, this self-assessment reflection revealed how I was purposed to serve the world with my gifts. Fourth, with my clear vision and gifts revealed, I wrote a business plan of action to share "Operation: One Focus" with the world. I contacted a former classmate and asked for her assistance with my vision. Remember, Jesus always sent disciples in pairs. I attempted various business ventures to finance my vision of empowering women and their families. I sought real estate investment, but, due to lack of substantial down payment and fear, it did not materialize. We wrote proposals to seek funding, but, due to intense competition, this also did not materialize. Lastly, I used my income as a substitute teacher to finance my God-given vision and created training and instructional materials (tools) then began to share workshops and seminars with businesses in my community as a gift. Thus, with continuous prayer, perseverance and courage, the One Focus Empowerment vision was beginning to become a visible reality. This new focus increased my confidence and it was carried over into my relationships. Finally, there was peace again.

Shortly after, I became pregnant with my daughter, Nia, whose name means "purpose." I experienced mixed feelings. I was overjoyed to be pregnant again because that's what I had prayed for, but I was fearful because I had just left my ten-year tenured job for a God-given vision/career plan. I experienced a very painful first trimester due to fibroids and an ovarian cyst. My mate experienced pressure because, for the first time, he had to handle the majority of the household bills. We were pressured for different reasons. I recognized the pattern. Due to physical and emotional turmoil, I could not be the positive catalyst I knew I had to be. However, I continued to pray and stay focused on my vision. The birth of our daughter made things peaceful again. Although the added responsibility again caused increased pressure, I felt that, with the birth of my daughter, I came full circle. The close mother and daughter relationship that I lost with the passing of the moment was regained. I was now more prayerful, powerful and peacefully empowered, thus more confident. Ultimately, I realized I had to let go of all the past growth-provoking experiences and simply forgive, press on and keep my focus on my God-given gift I am purposed to serve and share with the world. Also, I realized I cannot forgive by myself; I needed a higher power to help me forgive and look for the lesson.

~Fruits of Peace~

Purpose Discovery

1. Seek what you love to do…

Questions that will reveal who you love/enjoy:

- What do I spend a lot of time doing?
- What were my favorite subjects in school?
- What jobs/assignments did I enjoy? Why?
- What qualities did my favorite teachers or managers have?

2. Become an expert in the field…

- Expand knowledge/Create tools

3. Seek to serve others…

- Be a humble giver

Your PURPOSE / CAREER is your passionate lifework!

Remember, you too have a purposeful gift, but it can only be revealed and used if you free yourself and forgive. This will result in a peaceful existence. Also, hold onto hope for a brighter tomorrow. Remembering the words of my mom's favorite song, "Our day will come."

Reflection Exercise

Love keeps no record of wrongs...

I. Speak Positives - My Affirmation Statement:

Say aloud and write the affirmation statement 7 times.

"I am forgiving others so I can be forgiven."

II. Serve Self and Others - My Love Walk:

Love always creates inner peace!

Today, I walked in love via forgiving a family member, friend, coworker, etc.

Give personal example: _______________________

III. Relax/Meditate - Silent Moments of Connections:

Turn off the TV, cellphone, etc.

Write a gratitude statement about a person you have forgiven.

IV. Be Grateful - Gratitude Journal Entry: Fill in the blank.
"Today, I am thankful for _______________."

18
Peaceful Parenting: Love and Peace

Love is Kind…

Today's Working Definition: **Kindness:** actions that demonstrate concern for others.

This peace-provoking act requires us to understand ourselves as well as the nature of others. Although this section used one of the most significant relationships—parent and child—to illustrate, certain aspects of these life skills can be applied to other relationships as well. It focuses on agreement or harmony. Kindness is acting in a loving and giving manner. It is pleasant and helpful, not rude.

Oftentimes, when we think about our life's purpose, our thoughts are directed toward our careers or what we are supposed to do with our lives to live a meaningful life. However, purpose is the reason we were created. We were created to do more than just work. We were created to multiply and fill the earth, and to love. We are multi-purposeful. Thus, I believe my life's purposes consist of different roles—a mother, Career Technical Education (CTE) teacher, an educational leader, mentor and author. I believe these roles are my purposeful, earthly ministries.

So, my journey to kindness begins…

Parents give and receive the gift of love. Love is a source of joy, peace and increased self-confidence. As we journey through parenthood, the most important skill we need is to know how to show unconditional love. It is giving and providing an example of love that leads to peaceful parenting. A parent's love for their children should be patient, kind, not easily angered and forgiving (Corinthians 13:4). Therefore, we need to walk in love through our parental journey. This will result in peaceful parenting.

In today's generation, our busy schedules can often create a barrier to demonstrating high-quality parent and child relationships that are focused on harmonious interactions. However, we have to consciously allocate time to provide high-quality, patience-filled love interactions with our children. This is a very valuable, intangible gift we should give to our children. Oftentimes, we provide tangible gifts such as toys, clothes and money but it is the intangible gifts that are really needed and desired for our children's development. This act of providing time alone and sharing without rushing will produce positive behavior. On the other hand, if a child does not receive this attention, the lack could manifest into negative behavior.

Second, we have to be mindful of our communication style with our children. It should exemplify kindness, love, peace and respect. We need to watch how we talk to our children. He who holds his tongue is wise (Proverbs 10:19). We need to guard the tongue so that we do not respond rudely. This can damage our child's self-esteem, which can also lead to increased negative behavior. We need to use what I call "love handles," such as "please" and "thank you" when communicating with them like we would with anyone else. Oftentimes, we communicate this way in our workplace but do not think it is important at home when talking to our children. Also, we need to be slow to speak and quick to listen. Listening is a critical component of communication, which often is not emphasized. These acts will build your children's self-esteem by making them feel important and respected.

Third, we need to practice self-control, or not being led by our emotions (feelings), when responding to our children. We should remain calm and peaceful and pray for guidance when responding to immature behavior. In other words, we should not resist the urge to be easily angered. It's OK to feel angry. It is simply an indicator that something is not right, but we should not act negatively in anger. Remember, life is cyclical and an up-down change in behavior is only natural. In essence, we have to teach our children mental fitness so they can build up their resistance to negative stimuli and choose the appropriate response. This is self-control. We are all growing; therefore, self-control will involve demonstrating acceptance and peace.

Lastly, we should seek to quickly forgive our children as well as ask for forgiveness from them. We all are works in progress and to err is human. There are not any perfect parents, just loving examples of peace. Be mindful that children are simply growing and learning at a very fast pace. Have compassion and empathy because we should be aware that growth and learning can be overwhelming. We should feel free both to tell them we understand, and we will always forgive them, as well as ask them for forgiveness when we make mistakes. Communicate forgiveness!

It is my belief that, if we incorporate these acts of love, patience-filled quality time, kind communication, managed emotions and mutual forgiveness, our parenting experience will be filled with more peace. It is unfair for us to expect our children to display behaviors if we are not displaying them ourselves. Remember, we reap what we sow. This is the law of cause and effect. Keep in mind that peace empowers that parent and child to reach their full potential, or purposeful destiny, so seek harmonious interactions.

Reflection Exercise

Love

I. Speak Positives - Affirmation Statement:

Say aloud and write an affirmation statement 7 times.

"I am an example of peaceful love for my children."

II. Serve Self and Others - Parental Love Walk:

I demonstrated love to my child today by: _______________________

- ❖ Spending quality time together
- ❖ Communicating with kindness using "Please" and "Thank you"
- ❖ Practicing self-control, managing my emotions
- ❖ Forgiving and asking for forgiveness

My personal example: _______________________

III. Relax/Meditate - Silent Moments of Connection:

Write a love letter to your child. Include it in his/her school lunch box or book bag as a surprise.

*For younger children, use pictures, for example, a smiling face in different shapes

*For older kids, write a short note with words of love, encouragement, compliments, praise and gratitude.

IV. Be Grateful - Gratitude Journal Entry: Fill in the blank.

"Today, I am thankful for _______________________."

19

Peaceful Parenting: Self-Love

"Live a Life of Love"
(Ephesians 5:2)

Oftentimes, we focus on our children's or our partner's needs before our own. It is essential that we focus on inner beauty, or on cultivating a mind and heart that is filled with love, peace and joy. It is critical that we spend time refueling or renewing ourselves so that we are able to serve as examples of peace for our children. Parents need to practice daily acts of holistic renewal of self. This holistic renewal requires that we take time to participate in activities that will mentally, emotionally, physically, socially and spiritually rejuvenate self. When we are deficient in one of these areas, we cannot serve as an example of holistic or well-balanced living. In other words, we cannot serve as an example if we are not participating in holistic activities ourselves.

First, we need to be conscious to allow time to love ourselves. We have to walk in love and peace for our children. If we do not love or feel good about ourselves, it will often affect the people who we are closest to—our children. Therefore, it is critical to fill our love cup continuously so we can give it to our children as well as others, keeping in mind that we cannot give what we do not have. In other words, if we don't have love for ourselves, how can we give it to others?

Second, we have to be patient with ourselves, keeping in mind that there are no perfect parents. Our aim should be simply to utilize parenting skills that will result in peaceful parenting. When we error, and we will, we should simply ask our children for forgiveness. Remember, we are all works in progress. It's OK. We are not bad parents because we occasionally have a negative response to our child's negative behavior. However, we need to be conscious that it is not excessive or uncontrollable anger-based reactions; if it is excessive, we should seek counseling or guidance. Oftentimes, this is a sign that it is time for parental self-love. Primarily, our goal is to seek to have balance and peaceful reactions with our children. If there is an imbalanced situation, we should lean toward a positive, proactive response instead of negative, reactive responses.

Third, we should be kind to ourselves and encourage ourselves with positive affirmation statements. As stated earlier, an affirmation statement is an act that emphasizes the power of words. Remember, the earth and everything in it was created by the spoken word (Genesis 1-2). Consequently, I begin each reflective exercise with a positive affirmation statement. Here are some examples: "I am a good parent." "I will practice showing peace and love to my children daily," or "I am a daily example of peace." These statements can be cited aloud or silently at the beginning of each day. When a child is displaying negative behavior, saying the affirming statements can give you a sense of peace and calmness so your response is proactive instead of reactive. This display of self-love will have a profound impact on your parenting experience.

In addition, we need to take some time to work on outer beauty or pamper ourselves with beauty treatments, manicures, pedicures and massages. However, be mindful that pampering can also include any holistic activity that brings a feeling of inner peace and joy. Thus, pampering ourselves gives us inner peace that can often manifest outwardly. Because time is often limited because of our many responsibilities, we can make our daily hygiene "special" by including candles, incense and oils with your favorite scents when bathing. I use chamomile, jasmine and lavender essential oils because they have calming and soothing properties. Plan your own self-pampering rituals. Also, if your budget permits, buy yourself a new outfit. A happy parent creates happy children because energy is transferable.

In one of my "Pampering Self" workshops, one of the participants stated that the information shared resulted in greater awareness of the importance of self-love. Also, she stated she was implementing more pampering activities into her lifestyle, and, as a result, she was more patient with her children. So, mom what are you waiting for? Get busy filling your love cup!

Although inner beauty is far more important than outer beauty, both are essential for peaceful parenting. So, go ahead and treat yourself. The best gift you can give your child is a self-loved, peaceful, pampered, relaxed, stress-free parent. Remember the words of one of my favorite quotes, "To thine own self be true" - William Shakespeare.

Reflection Exercise

Self-Love

The Power of Words:

I. Speak Positives - Affirmation Statement:

Say aloud and write the affirmation statement 7 times.

"I daily take time to fill my love cup and pamper myself."

II. Serve Self and Others - Parental Love Walk:

I demonstrated self-love by reading inspirational literature this morning.

My personal example: ___________________

III. Relax and Meditate - Silent Moments of Connection:

Turn off the TV, cell phone, etc.

I spent time today pampering myself.

Engage in an activity you enjoy that brings you inner peace; for example, crocheting, knitting, watching videos of your favorite YouTuber, etc. Treat yourself to a manicure or pedicure.

IV. Be Grateful - Gratitude Journal Entry: Fill in the blank.
"Today, I am thankful for ___________________."

20

Peaceful Parenting: Acceptance

"When I was a child, I talked like a child, I thought like a child, and I reasoned like a child..."
(1 Corinthians 13:11)

Parents cultivate the peace-filled gift of acceptance. Acceptance is a peaceful gift we give to those we love. In God's parental example, we see from the beginning that Adam and Eve did not listen when their father told them not to eat from the forbidden tree. They were disobedient. Also, the Israelites often complained (whined) and forgot to be thankful for the things their father provided. Do these acts—not listening, disobeying and complaining (whining)—sound familiar? As parents, we are all too familiar with this kind of behavior from our children. Oftentimes, we become angry when this behavior is exhibited because we feel that our children forget the sacrifices, we make for them. Be mindful. It is OK to get angry; this kind of behavior angered God also, but we should follow our heavenly example and provide them with a peaceful and loving example of compassion and forgiveness. We simply need to accept these behaviors as common and be mindful of our response to them.

I believe we need to change the way we look at negative behavior and simply consider it as growth-provoking behavior. The negative, growth-provoking behavior is often displayed in two forms—speech and action. Here are some examples of negative speech: complaining (whining), disrespectful back talk, negative self-take, name calling, lying and cursing. In essence, these growth-provoking behaviors are the result of choosing the wrong decisions in words and/or actions. When we see these behaviors manifest, they should serve as signals that love and attention are needed.

We need to develop a plan of action that includes peaceful tactics to help our children express themselves in positive ways. First, we need to pray for them as well as for ourselves so we will have the right response. Second, we need to encourage and validate their feelings. Third, we should ask our children questions about their negative behaviors. Lastly, we need to reach out to them with an act of love. For example, we can give them a hug. However, depending on the seriousness of the negative behavior, punishment or discipline may need to be administered. I believe we should always let the child know what the punishment will be if the negative behavior continues, and it should be implemented immediately.

I used the 3-strike method of discipline. If the child does not listen to parental instruction and continues the negative behavior after 3 strikes or verbal warnings, the discipline will be implemented (again, depending on the severity of negative behavior; some actions only get one strike before discipline is administered). I will cover this in more detail in the next chapter. I tended to favor time-out over spanking when my kids were young because I believe spanking teaches aggressive behavior and it does not provide a peaceful example for our children to follow. When my kids were youngsters, their timeouts involved not being able to go outside to play with friends. However, as my children got older, their time-outs consisted of not being able to play on gaming systems or use cell phones. Both are extremely effective discipline strategies. Taking away playtime or electronics is a big deal to a kid; it appears to hurt more than a spanking. If we don't want our children to be physically aggressive, we have to exemplify the same behavior.

We need to accept the fact that we all are works in progress. Don't take the child's negative behavior personally. Remember, it is only natural. Simply pray, smile, remain calm and peaceful so you can be a loving example of powerful parenting. Keep in mind that all battles belong to God and, ultimately, your child belongs to God; we are simply stewards. We have been entrusted to help manage them by providing a peaceful example.

Reflection Exercise

Acceptance

The Power of Words:

I. Speak Positives - My Affirmation Statement:

Say aloud, and write the affirmation statement 7 times:

"I am accepting my child's behavior as natural, and I am choosing to respond in love."

II. Serve Self and Others - My Parental Love Walk:

- ❖ I demonstrated love to my child today by:
- ❖ Displaying affection—hugging and kissing
- ❖ Giving praise or compliments
- ❖ Rewarding positive behavior by treating their favorite restaurant, new outfit, tennis shoes, etc.

My personal example: _______________________

III. Relax/Meditate - Silent Moments of Connection:

Turn off the TV, cell phone, etc.

Sit down, look into your child's eyes and listen intently without interruption or criticism. Simply listen!

IV. Be Grateful-Gratitude Journal Entry: Fill in the blank. "Today, I am thankful for _______________."

21
Peaceful Parenting: Discipline

"Discipline your son and he will give you PEACE..."
(Proverbs 29:17)

Our children belong to God; we are simply to be stewards over them. This stewardship, or act of leadership, requires that we provide guidance by shaping our children's behavior to move in a positive direction using discipline. In other words, we are appointed to lead successfully along life's journey via discipline.

I believe the best way for a parent to train is to be an example of discipline or self-controlled living. Remember, the parent is the children's pride (Proverbs 17:6). We must practice self-control or self-discipline ourselves so our children can imitate it. Self-control is only possible if we detach from our emotions and feelings and choose positive responses to our children's negative behaviors. This is a proactive response. Consequently, when we detach from our emotions and feelings, we can bring about a peaceful transformation. This requires mental strength, which is developed by resisting our natural tendency to react to anger with anger. Parents should be conscious that anger is inner pain and anxiety that manifests itself outwardly in negative behavior. When we lose self-control and react negatively to our children's behavior, we have given them control. Be an example of self-control and do not give your peaceful power away.

In the beginning of my teaching career, when I was serving as a substitute teacher in the public-school system, I noticed some students' lack of discipline was a major concern for the teachers and administrators. The students desired to participate in negative behaviors—excessive talking, cursing, defiance, disrespect and excessive playing during instruction. Some students even skipped class by staying out of school or by walking the halls during class periods. Also, there was excessive tardiness, and some of the students did not acknowledge the bell for the start of each class and simply chose to enter their class leisurely at their own discretion. It appeared to some that students lacked respect for authority figures, teachers and school principals. Their words and actions often demonstrated that they lacked respect for education as a whole. Although the high school security team and School Resource Officers (SRO) helped to enforce school rules and policies, student self-discipline was still a serious issue and a distraction to the learning environment. As a result, these negative behaviors have resulted in a large volume of poor grades in courses and summative assessments. As I stated earlier, not all students exhibit these negative behaviors, but there appeared to be a significant number of students at risk at schools where I taught.

I had not been in the K-12 public school environment in approximately two decades since I graduated from high school, so I encountered a rude awakening because, when I was in grade school, a large majority of students respected their teachers and school administrators. Initially, the disobedience, defiance, lack of control and lack of respect for education shocked me. I encourage all parents to volunteer and spend a day at his or her child's school to actually witness the student's behaviors personally. Thus, we should encourage our children to exhibit the right behavior and choose not to be led by their negative feelings or the negative behaviors of their peers. We have to do our part and be an example of self-control. Talk to kids to determine their concerns and spend quality time giving them the attention they need and desire. This will help foster self-control in our children and, ultimately, in our schools.

Consequently, throughout Proverbs, the book of wisdom, the parental advice given to parents is primarily to discipline and train the child in the way he or she shall go. The advice given to the children is to listen to their parents and obey their teachings and instructions. Discipline is an act of love! It serves as an act of guidance. Discipline produces children exhibiting the right behavior. In addition, it provides peace for children who have been trained by it as well as peace for parents. Therefore, it is extremely important in raising and caring for our children. Often, when we hear, "spare the rod, spoil the child," we think of physical discipline, but I believe the rod is also symbolic of firmness, straightforwardness (not wavering) and consistent discipline, "mental discipline". Therefore, the discipline can be either mental or physical.

As I mentioned earlier, I used the 3-strikes method of discipline with my children. I believe this method serves as a proactive means of discipline instead of reactive. It acts as a buffer so that we do not act out of anger but out of peace and love. If we act out of anger, it will hinder peaceful relations between the parent and the child. This 3-strike method allows us time to choose our disciplinary response and allows the child an opportunity to choose the correct behavior by themselves. Therefore, it is an empowering act of discipline for our children. First, I give a verbal warning (strike 1). Second, I question my child about the behavior and let him/her know the consequences or punishment if the negative behavior continues (strike 2). Third, I implement the firm punishment that was previously announced immediately following the continuous disobedient act (strike 3). The discipline or punishment for the third strike is usually time-out of some sort, which I call the "mental rod". However, occasionally, depending on the seriousness of the behavior, i.e. if it is life-threatening, I may be punished with what I refer to as the "physical rod." For example, if when my child was young, he or she attempted to touch a hot stove, I may physically move their hand to protect them from being burned. My preference and routine of discipline was time-out because it gave the child time to think about their behavior and the consequence or punishment. It also allows them time to make the connection between the two. I believe this too is an empowerment act of discipline.

Discipline is an act of love and it produces good character. Although, at the time, your child may not see the benefits of it. We are to be a parent first and a friend second. Ironically, often, as parents, we do not see the benefits of hardships (discipline) in our lives. We also need to make the connection between behavior and consequences and seek the lesson to be learned. Remember, discipline builds character. The Bible encourages us to rejoice in our suffering because we know suffering produces perseverance, perseverance produces character and character produces hope (Romans 5:3, 4). Consequently, the purpose of discipline is to move children as well as ourselves toward our purposeful destiny.

Reflection Exercise

Discipline

The Power of Words:

I. Speak Positives - My Affirmation Statement:

Say aloud and write the affirmation statement 7 times.

"I am an example of self-love and self-discipline for my children."

II. Serve Self and Others - My Parental Love Walk:

I demonstrated love for my child today by choosing not to respond based on angry feelings (emotions) to my child's negative behaviors (complaining, whining, etc.) but respond from a place of love by…

My personal example: _______________________

III. Relax/Meditate - Silent Moments of Connection:

Turn off the TV, cell phone, etc.

Discuss with your children the purpose of discipline. Define and explain.

Also, devise a list of rewards together to reward positive well-disciplined behavior.

IV. Be Grateful-Gratitude Journal Entry: Fill in the blank. "Today, I am thankful for _______________."

22
Peaceful Parenting: Leadership

"*Those in authority should live peaceful and quiet lives...*"
(1 Timothy 2:2)

Parenthood cultivates the gift of leadership that requires a purposeful vision for our children's prosperous future. Leadership is letting our peaceful character serve as an example of influence. A purpose-based leader is aware that those that he or she is entrusted to guide are looking to him or her for guidance. Therefore, they pay close attention to their own behavior. True leaders are humble, like Moses; they know their position is not about their power or control but about their guidance by a higher power. Throughout Exodus, when Moses was constantly listening to complaining and seeing the negative behaviors of the Israelites, he always turned to God in prayer. Oftentimes, if we do not turn to our anchor, we will be overwhelmed by the negative behaviors of those who we are entrusted to guide and will be hindered from accomplishing our noble purposes or destiny. We will need help and it's OK! The most successful leaders asked for help and shared some of their responsibilities. Delegating different tasks is an essential component of leadership. Keep in mind, it takes a village to raise a child. Remember to include your higher power in your village.

After we accept our children's behavior as natural behavior. Keep in mind, we all experience mental conflict sometimes when choosing the right responses, and this includes children. They are simply little, fast-growing people. They get overwhelmed too. They are learning constantly about the world in which they live (school education) in addition to receiving character development instruction. Therefore, childhood can be overwhelming. We need to be conscious that negative behavior could be due to information overload. Consequently, it is critical to have a period of silence each day, such as nap time for little children, or encourage moments of silence for older children to unplug from electronics to recharge. Also, this is needed because peace gives power, and power leads to creativity. Ultimately, creativity will lead our children to fulfill their divine purpose.

I believe peaceful parents nurture the leadership potential in their children. It is our task as parents to encourage our children to think about how they would like to serve the world with their gifts. In essence, as parents and leaders of our family, we should encourage our children to have a vision, a future goal of how they want to improve the lives of others in the world. This is not only a critical characteristic of leadership but an act of empowerment. Here are some tactics to encourage children's gifts to manifest. First, allow children to make decisions and compliment them on their choices (even if you do not totally agree). For example, when my children were young, I allowed them to pick out their clothes for school, and when they graduated from high school, I encouraged them to pick their majors in college/career path. In both instances, I complimented them on their choices. As a result, both are confident, progressive adults. Second, ask them what they think about certain life experiences without criticizing their responses. Third, encourage praise, compliment them and let them know they were born to fulfill a divine purpose of serving others with their talents. This is leadership at its finest.

Mothers often believe it is our job alone to raise or take care of our children because, historically and globally, women have been the caretakers and nurturers of their families. However, I have found out that it is not solely our responsibility. The responsibility was meant to be shared, so moms take the pressure off. It is not your responsibility alone; it was intended to be shared with God, their father, co-parent, family and friends. Parents (mothers too) have many gifts, not just the ability to parent, and our children need to see and hear about us using those gifts as well. I believe that one of my gifts is to serve others by sharing information as an author, educator as well as a parent. When I share with my son my workshop experiences, he seems to be curious and enjoys listening to the participants' activities.

~Fruits of Peace~

Leadership

A true leader is an example of peace—a peacemaker
Peace brings transformation!
Leader Characteristics:

- They know they were born to lead

- They are vision-and-mission-driven

- They believe their life is a career

- They lead others to independence and self-empowerment

- They know the importance of their character (role models)

- They are led by inner spirit

- They are confident decision makers

- They are encouraging and inspiring in positive directions

- They are friendly, kind and humble (excellent interpersonal skills)

- They are great communicators, fully express themselves

- They are dependable and committed

- They are self-controlled and emotionally balanced

- They are fair and honest

- They are relationship builders

> ➢ They are innovative and creative

> ➢ They have a sense of humor

As parental leaders, we must have a positive and abundant vision for ourselves as well as children. We must communicate it and take necessary actions to ensure that our purpose manifests. Remember, it is our responsibility to lead by being a peaceful example. Being an example of a peaceful life of purpose will positively influence our children, and this is how we should lead.

Reflection Exercise

Leadership

I. Speak Positives - Affirmation Statement:

Say aloud and write the affirmation statement 7 times.

"I am leading by being an example of peaceful existence."

II. Serve Self and Others - Parental Love Walk:

I encourage the leadership potential in my child by allowing him or her to make their own decisions and choices, etc. (An act of empowerment)

My personal example:_________________________

III. Relax/Meditate - Silent Moments of Connection

Turn off the TV, cell phone, etc.

Encourage your child's creativity. Allow your child to create a vision board by printing and cutting out pictures that illustrate their dreams, goals and aspirations and glue the graphics to a poster board.

IV. Be Grateful - Gratitude Journal Entry: Fill in the blank.
"Today, I am thankful for _________________."

23

Peaceful Parenting: Holistic

Parenting

"I can do all things through Christ who strengthens me..."
(Philippians 4:13)

Parents are to be an example of wholeness or holistic living. In other words, we have to live as an example of balanced living. Holistic parenting focuses on the development of the whole child. It is not focusing on the problem or negative behavior. It offers a proactive approach to parenting. It focuses on the mental, emotional, physical, social and spiritual development of the child. In each of these areas, we must display behavior that reveals consciousness in each area. Mental/emotional holistic parenting includes programming positive thoughts as well as identifying whether the responses are thought, or emotion-based. Physical holistic parenting involves an awareness of our children's daily nutrition and exercise habits. Social holistic parenting focuses on the importance of relationships. Lastly, spiritual holistic parenting encourages the importance of community service.

Because of advances in technology, today's children are influenced mentally by an array of computer gadgets. This influence can be either positive or negative. Therefore, we have to filter out negative influences and filter in positive influences. Primarily, mental holistic parenting focuses on the child's thoughts and feelings. Our aim as parents is to help strengthen our child's mind by teaching mental fitness skills to encourage positive thinking and responses. The mind is a muscle, and muscles require resistance training. We need to teach our children how to resist the natural tendency to respond negatively to a negative stimulus. Don't take the bait. For example, we should discourage our children from reacting to anger with anger. The child should learn the consequences of reacting to anger with anger. The child should learn the importance of self-control. Essentially, our role is to serve as an example of positive thinking, speech and actions. Therefore, we need to be mindful of negative external influences that interfere with creating a positive mental attitude for our children. The sources of negative influences can be the TV, radio, Instagram, Twitter, YouTube, friends and the internet.

The trend of working mothers has increased the consumption of quick-fix processed foods like microwavable meals, chips and fast foods due to time constraints and convenience. As a result, childhood illnesses like latent diabetes are increasing due primarily to improper diet and lack of physical exercise due technology. There is a need for attention to physical holistic parenting skills. Physical holistic parenting focuses on the health of the child. Our aim as parents should be to make sure our children are getting proper nutrition and exercise to strengthen their growing bodies despite our busy schedule. As always, it is our responsibility to serve as an example of the proper nutrition and exercise by our habits. Also, with the invention of cellphones and video games, our children are becoming sedentary, which can lead to obesity and other illnesses. Being aware of this trend, we need to be examples of physical fitness and communicate its benefits. The benefits include increased self-esteem due to chemicals released during exercise, which makes us feel better. Physical exercise serves as a source of enjoyment or a hobby. Also, it increases oxygen to the brain, which results in increased cognitive ability. Last but not least, we need to exemplify and encourage the importance of grooming. Often, people judge us by our speech and our appearance. Consequently, good grooming also increases our children's self-esteem. In essence, we should be teaching our children to have an appreciation for their bodies.

Often, if the weather permitted, when my son was young, we would go to the park in the evening after work. He would ride his bicycle while I jogged along. Later, I had to decide how we would continue our trips to the park with the new addition to the family, his baby sister. Consequently, I pushed her in the stroller while I jogged, and my son rode his bike. My son would yell, "Mommy, you can't catch me!" It was truly a win-win as both parent and child were getting exercise and having fun at the same time.

However, when my son turned five years old, I placed him on a basketball team at a progressive church in our community. He met new friends in his teammates. My daughter met new friends in his teammate's siblings, and I met new friends in his teammate's parents. It was truly a joy-filled experience for all. This was only the beginning; my son went on to play tennis, soccer, baseball, football and basketball for different recreational teams in our community from the age of five until the age of seventeen years old. In addition, my daughter was a cheerleader, ballerina and served in her school's choir; she loved to sing from the age of four until thirteen. Although, oftentimes, there was a lot of running around for me with transporting my children to the different practices, games and activities. My work schedule as a high school teacher helped a great deal as I kept my children physically active. Also, I would walk and jog during their practices and attend aerobic classes. In summation, a physically holistic parent eats a proper diet, exercises and practices good grooming habits for their children to imitate, despite their hectic 21st century demands. Remember, body maintenance is critically important to children as well as our mental health.

We live in a culture that emphasizes the acquisition of material wealth; however, the route to wealth is often misleading. Social holistic parenting increases the awareness of the importance of social interaction or relationship-building as a means of acquiring success. First, we need to teach our children that wealthy people are leaders, not followers, who have a vision about how they are going to improve the lives of others. Second, we need to share with them that the way to wealth or success is by developing good relationships based on mutual respect and trust. Thus, developing good relationships often leads to success, along with technical skills. There are a lot of people with technical skills, e.g. college degrees, who are not wealthy or successful. On the other hand, there are many people who do not have technical skills or college degrees who are very wealthy and successful. Third, we should teach our children that wealthy people are compassionate, giving and need fillers. Their primary focus is not money but the joy from using their creative gifts to make a positive change in someone's life. Thus, to improve the lives of others we have to cultivate social relationships.

A parent should be a peaceful example of one who fosters trust and mutually respectful relationships. We should have a positive self-image and encourage others to do likewise by using praise, compliments and encouragement. After all, no one in a good frame of mind wants to develop a close relationship with a negative, highly critical person. Wealth is having the means to maintain our needs and acquire some of our wants. Success is having the courage to give unconditionally to acquire wealth. Success is cumulative and it is not a quick fix. It is the result of repetitive effort—trying, trying and trying. Therefore, the key to developing friendships is exhibiting positive holistic characteristics while walking in love with others.

My family partakes in a lot of social activities, especially on the weekends. When my kids were younger, we would go to the park, the mall, birthday parties, gatherings with family and friends and different restaurants. The parties alone keep my kids' social life pretty busy. As they got older, they stayed socially active by participating in basically every sport between the two because I believe social interaction increases self-confidence. Ultimately, we need to increase our children's awareness that we are social beings, and their social endeavors and formed relationships often lead to connections that are essential for the manifestation of their life's purpose.

Often, the focus in this society is on "me, myself and I," therefore, we need to teach our children that being successful in life is really about service or helping others with our gifts and talents. Spiritual holistic parenting focuses on the importance of service. Consequently, as parents, we need to set an example of community service by taking the time to give back and help those less fortunate. This is the purpose of our existence. We need to assist in nurturing our children's gifts and introduce them to the importance of giving to others. Our aim should be to encourage them to give more as they mature into adulthood. Interacting with positive, inspiring people and books helps to reveal our gifts. Therefore, we should exemplify and encourage inspirational interaction.

When my son was younger, I would often ask him what he wants to be when he grows up. Sometimes he would say he was going to be a doctor so he can make people feel better, and other times he says he is going to be a policeman so he could protect people. Currently, he is a Cum Laude honors college graduate with a degree in Health and Physical Education, so I guess you could say he is helping people feel better by providing information about proper diet and exercise while protecting their health. So, his career path is a blend of both health practitioner and protector. To God be the glory. He developed a conscience of helping others early in his childhood.

~Fruits of Peace~

Positive Mental Programming

The Mind is a Magnet

Our inner thoughts attract and create our outer experiences and reality.

Two Critical Mental Programming Techniques:

1. **AFFIRMATIONS**

→ Positive self-talk

→ Self-fulfilling prophecy

→ Affirms - "It is so."

→ Should be spoken with conviction and authority

2. **VISUALIZATIONS**

→ Forming a mental picture in the mind

→ Day/Night dreaming about a desired result

→ Take every negative thought captive immediately in mid-sentence and replace with a positive thought

→ Create and view your vision board daily

Use your mind to HEAL, INSPIRE and CREATE positive conditions and surroundings

Remember, our goal is to encourage mental, emotional, physical, social and spiritual fitness in our children so they can live balanced, full lives. So, get busy! In essence, holistic parenting will produce well-balanced, stable children.

Reflection Exercise

Holistic Parenting

The Power of Words

I. Speak Positives - Affirmation Statement:

Say aloud and write the affirmation statements 7 times.

"I am an example of mental, emotional, physical, social and spiritual wholeness."

II. Serve Self and Others - Parental Love Walk:

I demonstrated love for my child by:

Mentally (emotions) responding in love and anger

Physically preparing a well-balanced meal with fresh, organic vegetables

Socially complimenting my child on a job well done

Spiritually giving gifts to a non-profit community organization

My personal example: _________________________

III. Relax/Meditate - Silent Moments of Connection

Turn off the TV, cell phone, etc.

Go to the park and spend time doing what your child enjoys.

IV. Be Grateful - Gratitude Journal Entry: Fill in the blank.
"Today, I am thankful for ___________________."

24
Peaceful Parenting: Time Management

"There is a time for everything and a season for every activity under the sun…"
(Ecclesiastes 3:1)

As purpose-based leaders, life partners, parents, etc., the way we manage our time daily often affects our attainment of peaceful purpose. Practicing time management reduces stress and the possibility of becoming overwhelmed as we try to balance all our life's responsibilities. To manage our time effectively, we should set priorities or know the order of importance for the activities that govern our busy lives. We need to know what is important and what is not important. Oftentimes, we seem to get the two confused.

Again, I will use our role as parents to illustrate this purpose-based leadership skill. I believe our peaceful parenting activities, in order of priority, should be as follows: First, it is important to take the time to develop ourselves so we can provide a loving, peaceful example for our children. Throughout this guide, I have repeatedly emphasized in every act of parenting the need for us to be an example of desired behavior we want from our children. Keep in mind, what we do speaks louder to our children than what we say. Second, we need to take time to care for ourselves and for our children holistically. We need to allow time to make sure that we, as well as our children, are mentally, emotionally, physically, socially and spiritually fit. Third, it is important for us to take time for planning so that peaceful interactions can occur between our children and us. I was given a Stephen Covey planner at my first corporate job and I used one since. I use a planner to plan and write down pampering or self-love activities, holistic parenting activities, as well as to stay abreast of scheduled work and personal activities. I believe a planner is a peace-provoking tool. Lastly, it is critical that we allocate time to actually partake in activities that will involve doing something or spending quality with our children.

Likewise, we need to be conscious and limit time spent on non-important activities. These activities are often considered time wasters; for example, excessive TV/YouTube/Instagram viewing, social media, Facebook, Twitter, conversing, video game playing or lounging.

We need to manage our time using planning and organization skills to avoid peaceful interaction or prevent crisis. A crisis often occurs when we are rushed, for working moms who have to balance home and work responsibilities. Traditionally, women had domestic responsibility, primarily caring for the children and the housework. Today, all women working who try to manage both alone will often feel overwhelmed and stressed. This overwhelming feeling can often lead to crisis or peaceful interactions between you and your children. They want you! They don't care whether everything in your house is spotless. Therefore, peaceful parents of young children should concentrate on maintaining the essential areas, for example the kitchen and bathrooms.

When your children get older, you can share the housework with them. Start them young and teach them order and organization. Also, ask for help from your co-parent if one is present in the household. They can help by doing a house chore or by taking the kids out so you can do it effectively and efficiently. Remember, no one can work full-time, clean house and care holistically for their children and self without help. Keep in mind to ask for help and prioritize what is most important.

I will share a personal example to illustrate. In the morning, I was often rushing to get everything ready to go to work—myself, the kids, prepare breakfast and our lunches, etc. I'll start to feel overwhelmed or stressed, but when I planned and organized the night before, it helped the next morning run more smoothly and without any crisis or conflict, such as a child who does not listen or eat breakfast. With proper prioritizing and planning, my response was calmer and more peaceful, and I did not feel as rushed or overwhelmed. So, take the time to prioritize, plan and ask for help. Remember to allocate your time so peace can reign!

Reflection Exercise

Time Management

I. Speak Positives - Affirmation Statement:

Say aloud and write the affirmation statement 7 times.

"I am prioritizing my time to do what is most important for my children."

II. Serve Self and Others - Parental Love Walk

Take time to plan/write down daily activities and place in order of importance.

My personal example: _______________________

III. Relax/Meditate - Silent Moments of Connection

Turn off the TV, cell phone, etc.

Spend 2 hours (10% of 24-hour days) of quality time with your child daily. Write down the activity. Start an activity log for your kids.

IV. Be Grateful - Gratitude Journal Entry: Fill in the blank.
"Today, I am thankful for _______________."

25
Peaceful Parenting: Attitude of Gratitude

"Give thanks in all circumstances..."
(1 Thessalonians 5:18)

Through this purpose-based leadership program, we have journaled gratitude statements to empower us through this journey. Being thankful is a positive and uplifting mental practice that helps us successfully manage life's ups and downs. Consequently, being grateful for our rich relationships is essential for our purposeful journey. Remember, children are gifts from God. As peaceful parents, we need to focus on the gifts our children give. Therefore, we should not focus on the need to discipline negative behavior or the work involved in caring for our children. This negative focus will take away from seeing the gift of parenthood. The gifts they give are wonderful.

The gifts include the following: first, they are a source of joy and laughter. They are entertaining because children view life as a party. They enjoy dancing and singing. Sometimes, just sitting and watching them, you can't help but smile and laugh. They may even be able to teach you a few new moves. Oftentimes, on Saturdays, when my kids were young, we would watch a video on TV, dance and sing along with the videos. We would play with my son's drums and guitar. We would have a party. As I mentioned earlier, as my children got older, they would be all smiles when playing sports or participating in athletics, and I would be smiling and cheering them on from the stands. We had a lot of fun together. Try it. After all, the Bible encourages us to be childlike in spirit.

Second, children are a source of love. They continuously give love to their parents. This display of affection with lots of hugs and kisses helps comfort parents after a stressful workday. My mate and I enjoyed when we came in from work and the kids would run up to us and give a big hug, shouting, "Mommy" or "Daddy." As they get older, they may display affection differently because they are going through the phase when it's not "cool" to display parental affection openly, but they will display it in more subtle or cool ways.

Third, children are a source of knowledge. We can learn a lot from them, like how to love unconditionally with kindness and forgiveness. Oftentimes, when my son was younger, I would take him to the store for a treat, and he would say, "Mommy, are you going to buy a treat for daddy?" He used to say the same thing to his dad as well. One day, his dad came home with this apple paintbrush candy for me. It was kind and thoughtful, but the taste was, let's say, "interesting." As they got older, if I were stressing over something, my daughter would say, "Mom, God got your back."

Lastly, children are a source of motivation. They motivate and encourage us to work a little harder to supply for their needs and some of their wants. I often say they keep my hand on the plow, digging for a harvest for them to enjoy as well as a prosperous legacy for them to follow. For example, since my kids were born, I have completed my Post Masters certification and Doctorate in Educational Leadership as well as National Board Certification. Also, I have volunteered to start various educational programs and services and created curriculums for various business, marketing and Information Technology (IT) courses. In essence, our children give us a reason to persevere. Often, I look at them and think that I have to lead them by being an example of service to others. They're definitely gifts from above, so unwrap and enjoy.

As I have stated throughout this section, our gift to our children is being whole, or well-balanced, and an example of love, peace and joy. This requires us to be in the present. Oftentimes, when we are with our children physically—living in the same house—mentally, emotionally, socially and spiritually, we are not present. Our children don't need empty vessels; they need you to be totally in the present. We feel we need to work to provide for them materially. I have found this is especially true for some men. The need to provide financially is their focus. Not to say this is not important, but they need balance to become stable, productive adults. In other words, our children need us in the present and whole. Remember, being in the present is the best gift we can give our children.

Reflection Exercise

Attitude of Gratitude

The Power of Words

I. Speak Positives - Affirmation Statement:

Say aloud and write the affirmation statement 7 times.

"My children are continuously adding joy to my life; therefore, they are precious gifts."

II. Serve Self and Others - Parental Love Walk:

I demonstrated a grateful attitude by taking a moment to reflect and write down what I experienced with my child that brought me joy…

➤ Watching my child joyfully dance made me laugh and smile.

➤ My personal example: ______________________

III. Relax/Meditation - Silent Moments of Connection

Turn off the TV, cellphone, etc.

Create a moment of joy.

Creatively make an invitation with your child for a family party. Play music and Dance! Dance! Dance! Then write a thank you note to your child for attending.

IV. Be Grateful - Gratitude Journal Entry: Fill in the blank.
"Today, I am thankful for ______________."

26
Peaceful Parenting: Legacy

"Parents are the pride of their children"
(Proverbs 17:6)

One of the most important questions we should ask ourselves is, "How do I want my children or grandchildren to remember me?" Our parental legacy is a gift that our kids inherit. It can have a profound impact on their lives. We should be mindful of the legacy we leave behind. Our children are looking to us as a role model for life. Thus, we have to be careful that our thoughts, speech, behavior and overall character demonstrate a positive, peaceful example for them to follow and inherit. Most importantly, I believe we have to look at our attitude because it determines ours and their aptitude. Our desire should be that our children reach their highest potential; therefore, it is of utmost importance to be mindful of displaying a positive attitude with love, peace and kindness.

The first step to forming a peaceful legacy is to set a parental vision/goal for what you want to be remembered for at the end of your earthly journey and write it down. Your goal should be based on your strongest belief and value—love, e.g. peaceful parent and child interaction. This goal will become your personal parental vision statement. My vision is to improve the lives of my children by sharing love and information that help them to improve their lives as well as the lives of their children. Second, we need to identify and isolate any potential legacy prohibitors that may interfere with our desired goal. These legacy prohibitors can be negative, fear-based thoughts regarding home and work or, in other words, the constraints affecting the time we need to fulfill our legacy. Third, we need to develop a legacy plan of action. In other words, how do I plan to work on the legacy I want to leave for my children? For example, I plan to spend a couple of hours with my child daily listening peacefully to his or her daily activities without any outside disturbances, e.g. electronics. Lastly, we need to read our legacy vision/goal regularly and stay focused on the legacy we want to leave behind so we can move forward toward our desired goal.

I was given a wonderful mother and daughter journal as a gift from a friend. It allowed me to share with my daughter memories about my mom as well as my life's journey to adulthood. Also, it allowed me to share memories of my daughter's childhood with her. I believe it will be a precious gift for Nia when she gets older. In addition, I believe it is a tangible parental legacy gift. I enjoy reminiscing and journaling about the past and present. It really brings joy to my soul.

What I remember most about my mom is that she was loving, giving and encouraging. In the same way, I would like my children to remember me as loving, giving, encouraging and as one who lived her life's passion and purpose. Remember, we have to have a peaceful destination and a road map to follow to help guide us along our harmonious journey.

~Fruits of Peace~

The Peaceful Parent Recipe

1 Gallon—Love/Peace Example

4 Cups—Parental Love

3 Cups—Acceptance

2 Cups—Discipline

2 Cups—Leadership

1 Cup—Holistic Parenting

1 Cup—Time Management

1 Cup—Attitude of Gratitude

Pour in Love/Peace Example, Parental Self Love, and Acceptance and mix well. Briskly stir in Discipline. Sprinkle in Leadership. Layer with Holistic Parenting. Top with Time Management. Sweeten with an Attitude of Gratitude. Now, savor your legacy.

Reflection Exercise

Legacy

The Power of Words

I. Speak Positives - Affirmation Statement:

Say aloud and write the affirmation statement 7 times.

"I am leaving a positive legacy for my children to inherit."

II. Serve Self and Others - Parental Love Walk:

I will demonstrate love to my child by displaying a positive attitude.

III. Relax/Meditate - Silent Moments of Connection:

Turn off the TV, cell phone, etc.

Spend time alone journaling to cultivate the legacy you want to leave behind for your children.

IV. Be Grateful - Gratitude Journal Entry: Fill in the blank.
"Today, I am thankful for _________________."

Cumulative Reflective Exercise

Parental Wisdom

Please read the following parental Bible verses. Think about what the verses mean to you and how they apply to your parental experience. You may want to discuss the verses with your family members and friends. These Bible verses will give us insight as to what it takes to be a peaceful parent.

"Listen to your father's instruction and do not forsake your mother's teaching."
(Proverbs 1:8-9)

"Parents are the pride of their children."
(Proverbs 17:6)

"Train a child in the way he should go and when he is old, he will not turn from it."
(Proverbs 22:6)

"Do not withhold discipline from a child.
If you punish him with the rod he will not die.
Punish him with the rod and save his soul from death."
(Proverbs 23:13-14)

"A rod of correction imparts wisdom, but a child left to himself disgraces his mother."
(Proverbs 29:15)

"He who spares the rod hates his son
but he who loves him is careful to discipline him."
(Proverbs 13:24)

"Discipline your son and he will give your peace; he will bring delight to your soul."
(Proverbs 29:17)

Purpose Road

~Walking in Your Miraculous, Noble Purpose~

This section provides a synopsis of the key lessons learned and miracles witnessed once one's purpose has been found. It illustrates that, if we stay connected to Spirit and practice self-reflection/meditation, we will realize that every person and experience we encountered along our journey is directly linked to the fulfillment of our purpose. These connections and the truth of God's word become crystal clear.

27
Purposeful Lessons

"The Lord will fulfill his purpose for me…"
(Psalm 138:8)

The journey to finding our peaceful purpose is a rich learning experience filled with questions and answers. As I sought to find out my life's purpose, I learned a great deal.

So, the journey to walking my peaceful purpose begins…

First, I learned that *our purpose is not about us*; it is about serving others with our God-given talents and giving God praise. Consequently, our purpose, or the reason for our earthly assignment, is not solely about the manifestations of our dreams, goals and aspirations. It is about God's desire to have a world that mirrors heaven. Thus, if we are connected to God, our dreams, vision and desires are from our heavenly father, so they should be one in the same. Thus, the manifestation of our life's purpose requires a love walk, keeping in mind that "love is patient, love is kind, it does not envy or boast, and it is not arrogant" (Corinthians 13:4). I believe *arrogant* implies that this love walk is not all about us. Our purpose is about using our talents to serve others while living a life that exemplifies love. Consequently, I did not receive my vision regarding my life's purpose until I sought God through Bible reading and journaling after receiving countless rejection letters after applying for what I thought were purposeful positions in my career path.

As I stated in the *Peaceful Legacy of Light* section, we are multifaceted, thus my purpose is to improve lives by sharing inspirational information in my different roles. Although, often, when we think about our purpose, we primarily think about our role as a worker (career-focused) but our calling can be carried out using our different roles, for example, parent, teacher, leader, author, etc. I believe my purpose in these roles use the same as well as different tools to share information such as encouragement and financial support, creative workshops and seminars, online courses, books, instructional resources for Career and Technical Education courses, leadership knowledge and qualities, etc. Ultimately, I believe sharing information to improve lives is my life's purpose or earthly assignment.

Second, on the journey to finding my peaceful purpose, I learned that *my upbringing provided the seed from which my purpose will grow.* I believe my parents were handpicked by God to be my earthly guides/angels. As I stated in the *Discovery Lane - Discovering your Peaceful Purpose* section, I don't think it is coincidental that my mom was giving and loving or that my dad loved to read books in his pastime. Also, my ability to observe these characteristics and make the connection was not an accident. My parents' key attributes have been instrumental to revealing clues to my purpose. Ultimately, my vision/purpose of helping others by giving information I have acquired from books and my life experience to help improve lives is not a random act, it is part of God's divine plan for my life. We are truly products of our upbringing.

Third, I learned that *we have to spend moments alone journaling without any distractions to listen to our lives, to hear God's voice and to receive wisdom regarding our purpose.* In other words, we must be silent witnesses and observers along our journey to finding our peaceful purpose. Oftentimes, I use quiet moments to journal, self-reflect and meditate. It is through these moments that I receive the clarity to find answers to questions and issues encountered. Overall, I have found spending quiet time journaling or writing down my thoughts, prayers, ideas, etc. have provided charity as well as direction as I transition through my peaceful journey. I often refer to these moments as "light bulb moments" because it is as though the light shines and I can see something that was initially not visible.

Also, this practice of journaling provided me wisdom and the ability to make connections between experiences that initially appeared random, which is truly a gift. Consequently, it was through the practice of journaling that I realized that my God-given vision, One Focus Empowerment (OFE), a training and consulting company which was, in essence, an educational facility manifested. I was given the vision in 1999 when I was routinely reading the Bible and other positive self-help literature to find answers to my life's purpose. My vision consisted of creating an educational facility which would provide remediation/tutoring services for children and adult learners, certification training (workshops and seminars) and extracurricular activities such as basketball, dance, etc. so that children and adults will have a place to distress and tap into their creative expression. Overall, my vision included a holistic approach where my students would have an opportunity for mental, emotional, physical, social and spiritual healing.

Journaling one morning, I realized that I had been working in the area of my purpose for approximately twenty years. I worked for school districts that provided the same services that I have given in my God-given vision. The name may have been different, but the work and offerings (services) were the same. For example, the school districts provided educational services, courses and remediation tutoring for children during the day and adults in the evening as well as extracurricular activities like basketball and dance. This journaling activity revealed the truth that I did not realize because I had not connected the two—my business/vision and my current assignment in the area of education. I was so grateful that, all along, God had been guiding, protecting, fortifying and blessing me and my children as I walked in my purpose. The ability to make connections is a gift that I am truly grateful for. So, get started praying, seeking God, journaling and you will be living a life of purpose. Be sure to use *One Focus Purpose Discovery Journal,* and you will acquire a more positive perspective of your life's purposeful journey.

Last but certainly not least, along my journey to finding my peaceful purpose, I learned that *adversity, or growth-provoking moments, and problems are inevitable, necessary and purpose drivers.* They shape our character in a noble Christ-like image, which is critical for lasting leadership. Although we do not like them because they don't feel good, they provide the most profound learning experiences. As I stated in the *Adversity Turnpike - Grieving the Sunset* section, the loss may come in different forms; for example, loss of a loved one, job, income, joy, peace, etc. However, the grieving and healing process is the same. The good news is, if we implement the holistic stress management strategies outlined in this book; for example, eating a proper diet and exercising (physical holistic learning), etc., we can not only survive the loss, but grow to a higher level as a result of the adverse situation.

Reflection Exercise

Purposeful Lessons

The Power of Words

I. Speak Positives - Affirmation Statement:

Say aloud and write the affirmation statement 7 times.

"I am living a prosperous, purpose-filled life."

II. Serve Self and Others - Parental Love Walk:

I will demonstrate love by writing and publishing books to share inspirational information that will improve the lives of others.

III. Relax/Meditate - Silent Moments of Connection:

Turn off the TV, cell phone, etc.

Spend time alone connecting with inner spirit (prayer/meditation), journaling and reflecting to gain insight in regard to the details of your purpose.

IV. Be Grateful - Gratitude Journal Entry: Fill in the blank.
"Today, I am thankful for ___________________."

Cumulative Reflective Exercise

~Fruits of Peace~

FOCUS UP SO YOU CAN RISE UP

FOCUS UP when your...

Career is unfulfilling

Money is decreasing

Love relationships appear to be diminishing

Children are misbehaving

Family members are ostracizing

Coworkers are politicking

Then you will **RISE UP!**

FOCUS UP is choosing to...

PRAY UP

PRAISE UP

WORSHIP UP

GIVE THANKS UP

BELIEVE UP

Keep your mind **FOCUSED** on God's promises revealed through his **WORD**, despite the illusion of self-limitations, adverse conditions and unjust situations so you can **RISE UP** to your **PURPOSEFUL POSITION.**

28
Purposeful Miracles Observed

"Your word is the truth"
(John 17:17)

Once you find your peaceful purpose, the reason you are here on a special assignment, the learning process does not stop, but you are now equipped with your passionate vision and survival tools to navigate through the inevitable losses/adversity that are inherent to your journey. Keep in mind, discovering your purpose is the first step, but maintaining it is another. For example, finding a mate or significant other is one step, but maintaining a strong, lasting marriage is another essential part of the journey.

God or the universe (whatever you choose to call the source) will send unexpected, positive occurrences to help you endure the inevitable ebbs and flows of this journey. You will experience miracles, unexpected divine events, so you will know you are aligned with God's purpose for your life. In essence, you will witness God's word being revealed through your life. In this last section, I will share personal examples revealed to me along my purposeful path. His amazing grace is wonderful to witness.

Purposeful Life Event 1

First, as I stated previously in the *Adversity Turnpike - Grieving the Sunset* section, my mom passed on in 1994 due to pancreatic/liver cancer. This was a devastating traumatic loss for me because she was more to me than just my mom; she was my best friend and the sister I never had.

Miracle-Truth Revealed

Shortly thereafter, I received two beautiful, healthy children, who are definitely gifts from God. My son, Johnny, which means "God is gracious" and a daughter, Nia, which means "Purpose." I believe I have received spiritual healing (grace) and purpose from these blessings because there are no coincidences, just divine occurrences. Word made flesh—instead of former shame (feelings of distress). "You will receive double portion..." (Isaiah 61.7)

Purposeful Life Event 2

Second, my marriage ended, and the kids and I were evicted from our family home. Shortly after, I stepped out on faith and I left my job of ten years to start One Focus Empowerment, an educational facility to share information that will improve the lives of others. This loss was heartbreaking too.

Miracle - Truth Revealed

Shortly afterwards, I received a brand-new home in a beautiful, suburban neighborhood that is in a high-quality school district for my children to attend. In addition, I finally received a full-time position in my purpose career path, education. It was truly a miracle for a single mom to purchase a new home with an income of 20K while working as a customer service call center representative. Again, the truth of God's word, "You will receive a double portion for your distress" (Isaiah 61:7) was revealed.

Purposeful Life Event 3

Third, I experienced a substantial financial loss and my close first cousin, who was like a little brother, passed away suddenly. Both losses were overwhelming and emotionally draining, but I keep pressing and walking in my purpose. Also, it was hope and positive expectations that things would get better according to God's promises that kept me.

Miracle - Truth Revealed

A little later, I was unexpectedly transferred to another school because the student enrollment decreased and, by God's favor, was offered a leadership position. The mere fact that all these occurrences were out of my control, but a positive outcome occurred, was God's grace and mercy in full effect. Not only did I receive a promotion, but the purposeful position was near my home, and, as a result, I could get to my kids quickly if they needed me because their schools were near. Again, God's word was made evident through my life, "double portion for distress" (Isaiah 61.7).

Purposeful Life Event 4

Fourth, I got demoted from my leadership position due to organizational politics. I could not reason or conceptualize why because my department was growing, and, as a result, we had to hire additional teachers and our students' credential assessment scores were outstanding. I was disappointed and perplexed, but another miracle was right around the corner.

Miracle - Truth Revealed

A little bit later, I received a position offer up north with an increase in salary. Also, I was placed in a position where I could share information to help more people because the IT program was innovative and offered skills for high-demand IT positions. As a result, other educational leaders from various states; for example, Atlanta and Baltimore, came to learn about the new specialty program. Also, by the grace of God, I received my doctorate degree in Educational Leadership. Another manifestation of God's word, "You will receive a double portion for your distress" (Isaiah 61:7) was made flesh though by my purposeful walk.

Patterns Reveal Truth

Currently, I am in the midst of walking through purposeful event five because I am experiencing a loss in income due to a shortened commute. After I received my Doctorate, I decided to try to find a position closer to home. The transition has been a difficult adjustment due to, approximately, a 20K decrease in salary. In addition, a pandemic recently occurred, which required people around the world to be quarantined but we already know the outcome. God does not change, "I/we will receive double for our trouble" (Isaiah 61:7), because "No weapon formed against us shall prosper" (Isaiah 54:17) and "We are more than a Conquerors" (Romans 8:31-39). Speak the truth over life and watch it manifest. Keeping in mind, this purposeful journey is not about us.

We all experience loss or adversity in our lives, be it a loss of a loved one, job, income, peace, joy etc.; however, the key is to practice the holistic healing strategies outlined in this book in the meantime, and expect a miracle based on God's word to manifest. It will. I am a living testimony to God's promises; they are always fulfilled. Remember, patterns always reveal truth!

God did not promise that living a life of purpose or meaning would be without adversities, but he promised a way of escape and an abundance of joy, peace and provision in the meantime. Enjoy the fruits of your purpose and leave a legacy of sharing your gifts to improve the lives of others. Miracles are common when you are walking in your purposeful assignment. Smile! We got this!

Cumulative Reflection Exercise

Vision Board

A Powerful and Purposeful Manifestation Tool

Create a vision board of what you desire for your life in the future. Keep in mind, a vision board is a visual that helps us to live a life of purpose. It is a powerful tool used to help clarify, concentrate and maintain focus on life's goals, dreams and aspirations. A vision board displays images that represent whatever you want to be, do or have in your life.

To determine what images and words you need to include in your vision board, consider the following questions...

A. **Your vision statement:** How do you want to serve the world with your gifts, talents, skills and abilities? Ex. vision statement: "To improve the lives of others by sharing inspirational information through books, workshops, seminars and conferences as courses."

B. **Your Pain**: What has been a continual source of pain in your life? Our purpose/vision is tied to our pain or the losses we experience along our life's journey. Ex. pain and suffering experienced due to the quest to find a position of purpose in my career.

C. **Your Values**: What is really important to you? Ex. rich relationships, a purposeful career, helping others, abundant resources, etc.

D. **Your Inner Spirit**: How you do want to feel when the things in your vision board are manifested? Ex. Joyful, Peaceful, Loved, Fulfilled

Okay, Let's Get started…

1) Find inspirational images and words aligned with your desires

2) Add to your vision board

3) Put your vision board somewhere that you can view it daily

4) Take actions that are aligned with your vision

5) Watch the vision become reality.

Cumulative Reflection Exercise

Purpose Terminology

Throughout *One Focus, The Journey to Finding Your Peaceful Purpose,* I have used several descriptive words to describe my journey to discovering my purpose—empowered living. Some of these words and their meanings must be shared with you to help you understand their meaning and how they may apply to your life on your path to empowerment through faith, love, as well as your life's choices. Please read these words and their intent. Apply them in your life as you continue in this guided journey to empowerment and purpose. Define the purpose-driven words in your own words. Make your definitions personal. Here are some examples:

Purpose: One's reason for being, or life's meaning. A unique gift to be shared with the world to improve the lives of others.

Empowerment: My God vision-based ability and personal power within to overcome trials and transitions. It moves me toward my purposeful destiny. I am able to tap into the power through faith in God and prayer.

Inner Peace: My ability to remain calm despite external situations. It allows me to be proactive and make good life choices as well as to be creative in pursuing my life's purpose. It is pure joy.

Confidence: My firm belief that I have the power within to determine the course of my life. It is trust in God.

Fear: False information that appears to be real. It can hinder or delay us from realizing and walking in our purpose.

Vision: A God-given goal that is directly linked to how we are to serve others with our talents.

Terms to Define:

- Anger
- Anxiety
- Balance
- Behaving
- Belief
- Change
- Communication
- Consequences
- Decision
- Demonstrate
- Depression
- Desire
- Emotional
- Encouragement
- Endure
- Ensuring
- Existence
- Faith
- Focus

- ➤ Foundation
- ➤ Healing
- ➤ Holistic
- ➤ Inspiration
- ➤ Love
- ➤ Need
- ➤ Overwhelmed
- ➤ Peace
- ➤ Personally
- ➤ Professional
- ➤ Purpose
- ➤ Rejection
- ➤ Spiritual
- ➤ Stress
- ➤ Transitioning
- ➤ Trooper
- ➤ Truth
- ➤ Vision

~Fruits of Peace~

The 7 Ps of Purpose

1. **Prayers**

2. **Past**

3. **Pain**

4. **People**

5. **Pleasure**

6. **Passion**

7. **Peace**

Every situation, adversity and person we encounter along this journey is purposeful. Each reveals clues that lead us to our purpose-sacred contract. Remember, life is simply a university of learning. Therefore, 99.9% of our lessons are attached to our purpose. There are no failures; we simply repeat life's tests until we discover our spiritual assignment. Each lesson learned results in a test passed or a promotion upward. It propels us upward to our realization of our spiritual purpose—total fulfillment. Ultimately, the lesson is for us to surrender our problems, or growth-provoking situations, to spirit. When we reach our purpose, we will reign with joy, peace, confidence and abundant prosperity.

CONCLUSION

One Focus: The Journey to Finding Your Peaceful Purpose is a unique inspirational and educational tool that answers the critical question: *how to discover and successfully walk in one's life purpose*. It illustrates the process of discovering one's life's meaning. All of life's journeys we travel consist of twists and turns as well as hills and valleys. Therefore, I used the physical journey throughout this book to illustrate the spiritual journey we must travel to fulfill our purposeful journey. First, I have shared the directions we must adhere to so we can reach our life's purpose: head North on *"Discovery Lane,"* turn left onto *"Adversity Turnpike,"* turn right onto *"Positivity Boulevard,"* take a right turn onto *"Sunshine Parkway,"* merge onto *"Relationships Highway,"* then turn right onto *"Purpose Road."* Now you have arrived at your destination. Second, to help you endure your journey, I have included some delicious treats, *"Fruits of Peace,"* to help nourish and sustain you along the way. Lastly, I have provided rest stops, *"Reflection Exercises,"* to ensure that you maintain visibility, clarity and guidance as needed along your sojourn. Keep in mind, once you have arrived in your purposeful position, the same practices introduced along the way must be continually implemented to maintain and secure your purposeful assignment.

In addition to the above conditions, along this inspirational journey, you will encounter travelers, who are essential to your ability to reach and maintain your life's purpose. The travelers I introduced along my purposeful journey were my parents, significant others and my children. In this book, I share my experiences with immediate family because I believe their influence is the most influential. However, there were other travelers who were instrumental in helping me reach as well as maintain my purpose, for example, teachers, professors, mentors, extended family members, friends, as well as coworkers. Remember, one's purpose cannot be fulfilled without personal relationships, so be grateful for these travelers because they serve as guides to help you along your purposeful journey.

As I shared earlier, our purpose is a multifaceted and vision-driven experience that includes all of our roles. For example, my vision to improve the lives of others by sharing inspirational information is fulfilled in my role as a parent, friend, teacher, career coach, facilitator and author. Be mindful that our vision extends to all areas of our lives; it is not limited to your occupation or work. Therefore, consciousness of family-work balance is essential along the journey.

Keep in mind, there will be instances when your purposeful journey is transitioning to a higher terrain which will be indicative of a period of stagnation, or in a holding period, but stay the course. Expect a miracle to appear and your purpose's vision will manifest. *"Your vision will come at the appointed time, it will not lie, though it lingers, wait for it, it will surely come and not delay" (Habakkuk 2:2-3)*. In the meantime, when you incur inevitable losses and grief along the way, remember to insulate yourself with the holistic spiritual, mental, emotional and physical healing practices and stress management techniques detailed in this book, and you will endure until a purposeful journey reaches its new, higher level.

Now that you know how to discover, prosper in the meantime and maintain while walking in your purpose. What are you waiting for? Your abundant purpose awaits you. Remember, my fellow travelers, to seek God through his word, speak positive affirmations, seek to serve self/others, practice stress management techniques, exercise, eat healthy, relax/meditate spend time alone journalizing and reflecting with a grateful heart, and you will walk confidently in true wealth and abundance along life's journey. You got this! Love, Dr. B.

<u>Empowering Bible Verses</u>

"If you seek first the kingdom and all these things (my desires) will be given to you."
(Matthew 6:33)

"No weapon formed against me shall prosper."
(Isaiah 54:17)

"For God has not given me a spirit of fear but a spirit of power, love and a sound mind."
(2 Timothy 1:7)

"I can do all things through Christ who strengthens me."
(Philippians 4:13)

"Whoso keepeth his mouth and tongue keeps his soul from trouble."
(Proverbs 21:23)

"Your word is the truth."
(John 17:17)

"Instead of former shame (distress) you will receive a double portion."
(Isaiah 61:7)

"Where there is no vision, the people perish."
(Proverbs 29:18)

"God speaks to us in dreams and visions."
(Job 33: 15,16)

"Write the vision, make it plain, it shall speak and not lie, wait for it, it will surely come."
(Habakkuk 2:2-3)

"If anyone does not provide for his own family first, he is worse than an unbeliever."
(1 Timothy 5:8)

"Those in authority should live peaceful and quiet lives"
(1 Timothy 2:2)

One Focus Empowerment Center (OFEC)

We at OFEC believe that "life is 10% what happens to you and 90% of how you respond" (Abraham Lincoln). I had this quote on my desk in my cubicles during my mom's passing and, often, I would say it as an affirmation statement. It encouraged me to respond to that challenging transition by maintaining a sound mind. It is our aim at OFEC to provide life skills and mentoring opportunities that will result in empowered, purposeful living.

For additional information, copies of the One Focus series books, workshops, seminars, online courses, purpose-based leadership, mentorships and other products. Email us at trenia.lb@gmail.com.